[Ee vate] Pie	72
Pickle Lemons —	72
Lemon Pickle —	73
White Sauce for Carp —	74
[Calves] feet Jelly —	75
Garlic Vinegar —	75
To preserve fruit	75
Pudding —	
Currie Powder —	
White Soup —	
Fish Sauce — Cp.t Austen	77
Orange Wine —	
Green Gooseberry Wine	80
Cheese Puddings —	80
Rage Puddings	81
	82
	83
To cure Bacon —	
Ginger Beer —	85
To Pickle a Pork	85
Make veal Soup —	85
To make Gravy or Glaze	85
	86
Fish Sauce — —	86
Bread Sauce —	
[Pound] Cake —	87
Toasted Cheese —	88

Solid Custard —	90
To cure Bacon	91
Noyeau —	92
Scotch Orange Marm.	92
Roots Crust —	93
Macaroni	92
Mock Oyster Sauce	94
To prepare Rice for sweet dishes	95
To stew Apples / fruit	95
Croquets of Rice	96
Apple Snow	97
Bread Puddings	
in Cups —	98

Martha Lloyd's Household Book

Martha Lloyd's Household Book

The original manuscript from Jane Austen's kitchen

JULIENNE GEHRER

Bodleian Library
UNIVERSITY OF OXFORD

JANE AUSTEN'S
HOUSE

NOTE Many of these original recipes, both culinary and medicinal, contain ingredients now known to be toxic and are not advised for consumption or use.

First published in 2021 by the Bodleian Library,
Broad Street, Oxford OX1 3BG
in association with Jane Austen's House
www.bodleianshop.co.uk

ISBN 978 1 85124 560 4

Preface, chapters, transcription and glossary © Julienne Gehrer, 2021
Foreword © Deirdre Le Faye, 2021
Images of *Martha Lloyd's Household Book* between pages 67 & 69
© Jane Austen's House
All other images, unless specified on p. 166,
© Bodleian Library, University of Oxford, 2021
FRONT COVER Paul Sandby (1731–1809), *At Sandpit Gate, July 1751*, Pencil, pen & ink and watercolour. © Royal Collection Trust/© Her Majesty Queen Elizabeth II 2020
BACK COVER Photograph © by Julienne Gehrer

Cover design by Dot Little at the Bodleian Library
Designed and typeset in 11 on 15 Baskerville by illuminati, Grosmont
Printed and bound in China by C&C Offset Printing Co. Ltd
on 140 gsm Chinese Golden Sun woodfree FSC® paper

British Library Catalogue in Publishing Data
A CIP record of this publication is available from the British Library

Contents

Foreword

Deirdre Le Faye

So many biographies have already been written about Jane Austen, and so many volumes of literary criticism of her works, that unless and until some more of her letters come to light, there seems to be very little left to say on either aspect. The next step, therefore, is to look at her outer circle of friends and relations in the hope of finding some information which will throw unexpected sidelights upon her life and writings. One member of this outer circle, unnoticed in the main so far, is her long-time friend and kinswoman by marriage Martha Lloyd (1765–1843).

Jane and Martha first met in 1789, when the recently widowed Mrs Lloyd rented Deane parsonage from Revd George Austen, bringing with her Martha and Mary, her two unmarried daughters. In 1792 the Lloyds left Deane for Ibthorpe, a Hampshire village some miles north of Jane's home in the rectory at Steventon. Five years later, Mary Lloyd married Jane's eldest brother, James. Following her mother's death in 1805, Martha joined forces with Mrs Austen, Cassandra and Jane, and lived with them in Southampton and Chawton. In 1828 Martha herself became part of the Austen family by marrying the widower Admiral Francis Austen. She became mistress of the large house he later purchased, Portsdown Lodge, located on the hills above Portsmouth.

Portrait of Jane Austen sketched by her sister Cassandra around 1810, when they lived with their mother and Martha Lloyd at Chawton Cottage in Hampshire.

The Chawton Cottage kitchen window overlooked the garden and provided light for the hired cook working inside. Climbing roses framed the entry in 2016.

In 1806 Martha brought with her to the Austen household a manuscript volume, probably started at Ibthorpe, which has become known to scholars as *Martha Lloyd's Household Book*, and which Julienne Gehrer has painstakingly transcribed and studied and now puts before us as an extra window—a kitchen window, in fact—into life in Chawton Cottage during those years when Jane was busy publishing her three earlier novels and composing her last three works. Many other household books survive, and some have been published, but most of them deal with the problems of managing and catering for very large establishments and great houses—and so give a biased view of domestic life in the Regency era. Martha's book, on the contrary, was compiled for a family of the Middling Sort, as the expression was—unpretentious households of the literate and cultured professional classes, not landed gentry and not necessarily very well off.

Nowadays we know that Jane Austen was a devoted daughter, sister and aunt, as well as being a great writer; but she was not brilliant at everything and it has to be admitted that she was not particularly domesticated. She was skilful with her needle, sewing her own clothes and embroidering very neatly, but housekeeping and cookery were not her forte. Her first experience of managing a household was in her Steventon days, in the autumn of 1798, when Cassandra was away staying with brother Edward and his family in Godmersham in Kent, and Mrs Austen was unwell and confined to her bed. This left Jane to take charge of the rectory kitchen and provide meals for her father and herself. Luckily their cook, Mrs Nanny Littleworth, was well experienced and needed little more than general supervision, and Jane assured Cassandra:

> I carry about the keys of the Wine & Closet; & twice since I began this letter, have had orders to give in the Kitchen: Our dinner was very good yesterday, & the Chicken boiled perfectly tender; therefore I shall not be obliged to dismiss Nanny on that account.[1]

A fortnight later Jane was able to boast cheerfully to Cassandra,

> My mother desires me to tell you that I am a very good housekeeper, which I have no reluctance in doing, because I really think it my peculiar excellence, and for this reason—I always take care to provide such things as please my own appetite, which I consider as the chief merit in housekeeping. I have had some ragout veal, and I mean to have some haricot mutton to-morrow.[2]

Later in the same letter she is planning to have next week an ox cheek with little dumplings. Another dinner was pease soup, a spare rib and a pudding, which Jane was not ashamed to set before an unexpected guest, Mr Lyford the local doctor, who had called to check on Mrs Austen's health.[3] However, during the Christmas and New Year season of 1806–7 Jane could no longer honestly claim to be a good housekeeper, had she wished to do so even in jest. There was an Austen family gathering in Southampton lodgings while their newly leased house in Castle Square was being made ready for their occupation; and as in all family gatherings strains and tensions were showing through the overall cloak of goodwill. Captain Francis was anxiously awaiting orders from the Admiralty regarding his next command, and his young wife Mary was already pregnant with her first child and liable to suffer fainting fits in consequence. Cassandra was once again away at Godmersham, spending Christmas with brother Edward and his large family, and Martha had gone to her sister Eliza Fowle at Kintbury in Berkshire;

in their absence there was room in the lodgings for James and Mary Austen with their toddler Caroline to be invited to stay for a few days. Unfortunately the weather was in general too bad for outdoor exercise, and James, who hated to be confined indoors, was bored and restless— 'his time here is spent I think in walking about the House & banging the Doors, or ringing the Bell for a glass of Water'[4]—whilst his wife was pointedly uninterested in any of the books Jane had chosen for the family's evening pastime of reading aloud. Jane's mother was, of course, hostess to the group, which meant it fell to Jane to plan the family meals and supervise the inexperienced cook in the lodging house—with difficulty and some lack of success, since a boiled leg of mutton was sent to table very much underdone. She wrote crossly to Cassandra:

> When you receive this, our guests will be all gone or going; and I shall be left to the comfortable disposal of my time, to ease of mind from the torments of rice puddings and apple dumplings, and probably to regret that I did not take more pains to please them all.[5]

Since Revd George Austen's retirement in 1801 and death in 1805, his wife and daughters had led a rootless life, moving from one rented house or lodgings to another; but at last in the summer of 1809 the Austen ladies, now including Martha Lloyd, left Southampton to settle in Chawton Cottage (as it was then called) on Edward Austen's Hampshire estate. The grounds of the cottage were bigger than they are today, and included a shrubbery and gravel walk around the perimeter, with hedges, a small orchard and good kitchen garden, a grassy lawn and flower beds. It also had a large courtyard with outbuildings but without such luxuries as an ice house or separate game larder or dairy house.

After settling in at Chawton, the ladies divided the domestic tasks between them: Mrs Austen, now aged nearly 70, handed over the reins of household government to Cassandra and concentrated upon her own favourite pastime of gardening, particularly attending to the kitchen garden—her descendants remembered that she planted and dug up her own potatoes, dressed in an old green smock frock like any farm labourer. Cassandra took charge of the soft-fruit bushes, flower borders and pot plants; and Jane prepared the nine o'clock family breakfast, keeping the keys to the tea, sugar and wine stores. After this morning task she was free to enter the world of her imagination, to update her first three novels in the hope of publication, and go on unhesitatingly to compose her last three. Martha now came into her element in supervising the kitchen and the cooking of all other meals, armed with her household book, whose recipes were tailored to use the produce of the cottage's garden.

In the summer of 1816 Jane was busy composing the happy ending of *Persuasion* and was even working on the last chapter, when both Cassandra and Martha simultaneously went away for several days in early July, and Jane had to take Martha's place in the Chawton kitchen, to the detriment, as she knew, of her creative imagination: 'Composition seems to me impossible, with a head full of Joints of Mutton & doses of rhubarb.'[6] She thought she had finished *Persuasion* and wrote 'Finis. July 16. 1816' on what was then the last page of manuscript—but later on added another paragraph and wrote 'Finis July 18. 1816'. However, as her family later remembered, she was still dissatisfied with this ending, feeling it was tame and flat, and so rewrote the last two chapters into the version as now published, finally completing the work on 6 August 1816. So it could be said that it was Martha's absence which was responsible for the weakness of Jane's first attempt to conclude her narrative, and it was Martha's return to the cottage which relieved Jane of the interfering household duties and allowed her to re-enter the world of the Elliot family and create Anne's great speeches on the enduring quality of a woman's love. We should all therefore give three hearty cheers for Martha and drink a toast to her memory, in her own favourite spruce beer, for helping, even though unwittingly, to give Jane's genius time and room to expand, and create a work of literary art which has survived undiminished for two centuries.

Preface

Martha Lloyd's Household Book is one of the few items we have from Jane Austen's closest friend. As Martha was an integral part of Jane's life, her recipe book is a highlight of the collection at Jane Austen's House in Hampshire. It is fitting that the book resides at Chawton Cottage, a place both women called home. Much of what we know about Martha is through Jane's letters and a few family reminiscences. But if we reread what has been written about Jane Austen we can catch glimpses of Martha Lloyd, who was often a figure in the background or just nearby. Included as a natural preface to Martha's household book is an extensive biography of Martha Lloyd. Knowing more of Martha's life leads us to a greater understanding of the deep friendship between Martha and Jane, a friendship that also included Jane's sister Cassandra.

My first visit to Chawton Cottage in 1996 piqued my curiosity about the woman behind the manuscript cookbook. In more recent years I began connecting Martha's recipes with the food references in Jane's letters. With entries for toasted cheese, orange wine, pickled cucumbers, mead and many others, Martha captured much of what Jane enjoyed at the dinner table. Recipe contributions from Mrs Austen, Captain Austen and Mrs Lefroy affirmed Martha's place within Jane's inner circle. In fact, Martha lived over half her adult life within the closely knit Austen family. Many of the names in Martha's book also appear in

Jane's letters. Some families—Fowle, Craven and Dundas—are actually more closely linked to Martha than to Jane.

It has been both a privilege and a delight to work with Jane Austen's House on this endeavour, and to realize our long-shared goal of publishing Martha's book. Former director Mary Guyatt and collections volunteer Sue Dell have been true collaborators, partners and friends through every stage of the project. Collections and interpretation manager Sophie Reynolds and retail manager Ashleigh Stimpson responded kindly and swiftly to a number of random requests.

From our first discussions with Bodleian Library Publishing, head of publishing Samuel Fanous and editor Janet Phillips shared our vision for a full facsimile edition of Martha's book. With colour reproductions of the manuscript, the reader can appreciate the words exactly as they flowed from Martha's pen, and then gain additional information from the annotated transcription that follows.

Freydis Welland, a descendant from James Austen's branch of the family, graciously allowed us to publish Martha (née Lloyd) Austen's 1828 letter from Gosport. Ronald Dunning, fourth-great-grandson of Francis Austen, provided perspective and helpful information on Austen genealogy. Photographer Steve Ellis visited Wymering churchyard to provide us with a photograph of Martha's headstone.

It was no small task to ensure that the final transcription matched every irregular spelling, inserted word and cancelled character in Martha's original manuscript. Credit for this monumental effort goes to veteran proofreader Joyce Jennings. Maureen Stiller, honourable secretary of the Jane Austen Society, shared advice for working with the organization's past reports. Colleagues in the Jane Austen Society of North America reviewed chapter drafts and made helpful suggestions, namely: Sheryl Craig, Elizabeth Steele and Linda Slothouber.

Finally, anyone writing on a Jane Austen-related topic must appreciate and recognize the invaluable works of Deirdre Le Faye. It has been my distinct honour and a rare gift to consult with the renowned scholar throughout this project. With her keen eye and quick wit, Deirdre would have provided good company for Jane Austen. This book has been improved by her contributions and I am sincerely grateful.

Postscript

About the time I was completing the manuscript for this book, I attended the 2019 Annual General Meeting of the Jane Austen Society of North America held in Colonial Williamsburg, Virginia. At the conference, Sue Dell presented a lecture on a recent project involving the coverlet made by Jane, Cassandra and Mrs Austen. One of Jane's letters sent from the cottage to Cassandra makes reference to collecting fabric: 'Have you remembered to collect peices for the Patchwork?—We are now at a stand still.'[1] The colourful patchwork might have been stitched while Martha and the Austen women lived together at Chawton Cottage. If so, Sue reasoned, Martha may have contributed to the thousands of tiny stitches. I thought Sue's observation created the perfect metaphor for Martha's life: carefully and closely interwoven with the Austen family history is the helpful hand of Martha Lloyd.

Patchwork coverlet handed down through the Austen family and said to have been pieced by Jane, Cassandra and Mrs Austen some time after 1810.

Dedicated to the memory of Martha Lloyd.
'—she is the friend & Sister under every circumstance.'
Jane Austen, 13 October 1808

Martha Lloyd
in her own light

A full appreciation of *Martha Lloyd's Household Book* begins with an introduction to its creator—the woman who befriended a young Jane Austen, shared a home with the famous author and later married into the Austen family. Like so much under the umbrella of Jane Austen studies, Martha's existence has been defined by her proximity to the great novelist. But the life of Martha Lloyd can be better examined when pulled out from Jane Austen's shadow and viewed in its own modest light.

If Jane were writing Martha's biography, she might begin with 'Which of all her important nothings shall I tell you first?'[1] Jane's references to Martha involve the usual female topics of household details, apparel, balls, shopping and dining companions. There are no great headlines in Martha's life story other than that she was Jane Austen's closest friend. But Martha was also a loving daughter, sister, aunt—and eventually a wife and stepmother. As such, she had many claims on the affections of those around her.

We can compare Martha Lloyd with some of the secondary characters in Jane Austen's novels. She supports the main plot and at times conveys critical information. Like Elizabeth Bennet's close friend Charlotte Lucas, she seems content with her circumstances. Like Anne Elliot's dear

Steventon Rectory, Jane Austen's girlhood home, which Martha Lloyd often visited in the period 1789-92. Pencil drawing from 1820 by Anna Lefroy, Jane Austen's niece.

schoolmate Mrs Smith, she is cheerful beyond expectation. Like Emma's former governess Mrs Weston, she gives helpful advice. Throughout her life, Martha's actions demonstrated reason, duty, empathy, gratitude, generosity and kindness. As Jane wrote to Martha, 'You are made for doing good, & have quite as great a turn for it I think as for physicking little Children.'[2] In large and small matters, Martha was there for others.

Early years

Martha Lloyd started life a full decade before Jane Austen, but there are many parallels between the women's early years. Like Jane, Martha was born to a respectable clergyman with a good position and a woman with aristocratic family connections. Her father, Revd Noyes (or Nowis) Lloyd, was vicar of Little Hinton in Wiltshire. Her mother, Martha Craven, was the daughter of Elizabeth Staples and Charles Craven, the twenty-first governor of colonial South Carolina. Charles was the younger brother of William, the 2nd Lord Craven, who was the Lord Palatine of the Province of Carolina in 1708. There were a few colourful stories about Martha's grandparents. Grandmother Craven was said to have a stern, tyrannical temper and was remembered as an unkind, severe mother.[3] Grandfather Craven was accused of financial malpractice and died in reduced circumstances. His widow remarried within a year of his death.[4] These events transpired long before Martha's birth and seemed to have had no effect on her life two generations later. Occasionally, the Lloyd family name was written 'Floyd', in an effort to replicate the Welsh pronunciation.[5] We know that Martha's mother spelled it that way.[6] Our Martha used the *Ll* spelling of her surname.

All the Lloyd children, Martha (1765), Charles (1768), Eliza (1767) and Mary (1771), were born in Wiltshire, but moved to neighbouring Berkshire when their father became rector of Enborne near Newbury in 1771. Both Wiltshire and Berkshire border Jane Austen's native Hampshire, to the west and north respectively. In the Lloyds' fourth year at Enborne, a coachman brought smallpox to their home, initially concealing his exposure to the illness. Mr Lloyd, all the children and many of the servants contracted the disease. Young Charles died at the age of 7, and Mary was left with significant facial scars.

Except for the tragic loss of their brother, Martha and her sisters enjoyed a relatively happy and typical upbringing in their parsonage homes. The girls were educated primarily by their mother, who taught them reading and spelling, but she hired a tutor for lessons in writing and arithmetic. Mrs Lloyd made sure her daughters practised needle-work daily and could knit their own stockings. More for amusement than necessity, Martha and her sisters learned spinning, weaving and lacemaking. Singing was part of the Lloyd home, and Martha and Eliza were remembered as having particularly good voices. All the girls took weekly dance lessons at nearby Newbury.[7]

The Lloyd children enjoyed visits with their cousins, the Fowles, who lived just 3½ miles from Enborne in Kintbury. Eliza married Fulwar Craven Fowle in 1788. When young, brothers Fulwar and Thomas Fowle were pupils of Revd George Austen at Steventon. The Fowle boys soon befriended Jane's eldest brother James. These connections probably introduced Tom Fowle to Jane's sister Cassandra. The couple became engaged most likely in 1795.[8] Their union might have brought the Lloyd and Austen families together. For a time, it appeared that Martha and Jane would each be sister-in-law to a Fowle brother. But Cassandra and Tom delayed their marriage for financial reasons. Unfortunately, Tom died of yellow fever in 1797 while accompanying Lord Craven as his personal chaplain on the campaign to the West Indies.[9] If not for this tragedy, the Austens and Lloyds could have forged their bonds much earlier than they actually did.

Move to Hampshire

A different yet significant death brought the Lloyd and Austen families closer, both physically and emotionally. Martha's father died in January 1789, causing Mrs Lloyd to find a new home for herself and her two unmarried daughters. It is assumed that her Fowle relations connected her with Revd George Austen, who had advertised Deane Parsonage for rent. By the spring, the Lloyds had moved to Hampshire and within walking distance of the Austen family home at Steventon parsonage. Martha (aged 23) and Mary Lloyd (aged 18) became fast friends with Cassandra (aged 16) and Jane Austen (aged 13) despite their age differences.[10] Martha soon employed her sewing skills for Jane. In return, when teenage Jane wrote her comic novella 'Frederic and Elfrida', she dedicated it:

To Miss Lloyd

My dear Martha
     As a small testimony of the gratitude I feel for your late generosity to me in finishing my muslin Cloak, I beg leave to offer you this little production of your sincere Freind

The Author[11]

iv (ult)

To Miss Lloyd

My dear Martha

    as a small testimony of the grati:
:tude I feel for your late generosity to me in
finishing my muslin Cloak, I beg leave to offer you
this little production of your sincere Freind

              The Author

The families surely enjoyed many hours in each other's company until James Austen's engagement to Anne Matthew prompted the Lloyds to vacate Deane. James was to take up the curacy at Deane and the parsonage would become the couple's new home. In January 1792 Mrs Lloyd arranged her family's removal to Ibthorpe, a house on the outskirts of Hurstbourne Tarrant and some 15 miles from Steventon. Instead of distancing the relationship, the separation had the happy result of encouraging visits and correspondence. Through Jane and Cassandra's letters, we hear often about Martha—and we know how much the women looked forward to seeing each other. We feel Jane's eagerness in her phrasing: 'Do not let the Lloyds go on any account before I return'[12] and 'I am rejoiced to learn from Martha that they certainly continue at Ibthorp.'[13] A survey of Jane Austen's extant correspondence reveals that nearly half of her letters have references to Martha—this includes the four surviving letters directed to Martha specifically.

Martha and Cassandra also corresponded with each other independently of Jane. There was an understanding that the letters would be shared openly among the three women. While staying at Ibthorpe, Jane wrote to her sister, 'Martha desires her best love, & will be happy to welcome any letter from you to this house, whether it be addressed to herself or to me—And in fact, the difference of direction will not be material.'[14] Jane's statement reveals an underlying trust between the Austen sisters and their mutual friend Martha.

All one family

Another family death brought the Lloyd and Austen families even closer. Anne Austen, wife of Jane's brother James, died in May 1795. James was left with their 2-year-old daughter Anna. After courting his

Jane Austen's dedication to Martha Lloyd appears opposite the opening page of 'Frederic and Elfrida'. The comic novella was written around 1789 and later copied into a notebook the author labelled *Volume the First*.

Ibthorpe in 2014, where Mrs Martha Lloyd and her unmarried daughters, Martha and Mary, moved in 1792. Martha and her mother lived here until Mrs Lloyd's death in 1805.

widowed cousin Eliza de Feuillide and Mary Harrison of Andover, James proposed to Martha's sister Mary Lloyd in November 1796. A welcoming letter from Mrs Austen revealed that Martha might also be headed to the altar. 'Tell Martha, she too shall be my Daughter, she does me honor in the request—and Mr W: shall be my Son if he pleases—don't be alarm'd my dear Martha, I have kept & will keep your secret as close if I had been entrusted with it; which I do assure you, I never was, but found it out by my own Sprack Wit—but as we are now all of one family, there is no occasion I should keep it any longer a secret from herself.'[15] Mrs Austen was quick to welcome Martha as a daughter, and eager to assume enough familiarity to mention Martha's heartfelt secret.

About this time, Martha was making entries in her household book. We can estimate that her work spanned most of the Ibthorpe years (1792–1805) based on the sequence of the entries and their contributors. (See 'Dating Martha's Work', page 48.) Clearly Martha made entries before 1798—and most likely around 1796. If so, then 'A receipt for a Pudding' in Mrs Austen's characteristically humorous verse may have been written for Martha around this time. The opening line, 'If the Vicar you treat', could refer to almost anyone—or we might speculate that the mysterious Mr W was a vicar. (See facsimile, pp. 7–9.)

We do not know when Martha's secret expectation of marriage to Mr W turned into disappointment, but a letter between Jane and Cassandra confirmed that Martha had finally recovered. 'I hear that Martha is in better looks & Spirits than she has enjoyed for a long time; & I flatter myself she will now be able to jest openly about Mr W.'[16]

The next months were busy ones for Martha. In November she stayed for weeks at Deane to help her heavily pregnant sister Mary with the birth of James-Edward Austen. A few weeks later, Jane expected Martha to be 'deep in the study of Medicine preparatory to their removal from Ibthorpe'.[17] It is possible that Martha anticipated travelling to Kintbury to help sister Eliza with new daughter Elizabeth-Caroline Fowle, born 6 December. This supportive role is one Martha had in common with Cassandra Austen, who was often in Kent for the births of brother Edward's eleven children. Martha's sister Eliza had eight children.

It is very clear that Jane and Cassandra shared concern for Martha's happiness. When Jane wrote to announce that their sailor brother Frank was on the cusp of a naval commission, she told Cassandra, 'Your cheif wish is now ready to be accomplished; & could Lord Spencer give happiness to Martha at the same time, what a joyful heart he would make of Yours!'[18] Jane's comment has led to some conjecture about the Austen sisters desiring a union between Martha and Frank, but we have no evidence to support this theory. Given the genuine, sisterly concern the Austens expressed for Martha, it is more likely that the comment fell along the lines of 'Now if only Lord Spencer could commission Martha's happiness as well!'

This sisterly affection was also demonstrated in temporary sleeping arrangements. Martha made room in her bed for Jane when they were at Deane for their nephew's christening. 'Nurse & the Child slept upon the floor; & there we all were in some confusion & great comfort;—the bed did exceedingly well for us, both to lie awake in & talk till two o'clock, & to sleep in the rest of the night.'[19] Scholars frequently note that little James-Edward would eventually become Jane's first biographer. We might assume that he and his little sister Caroline also enjoyed a close bond with their equally related but less famous Aunt Martha.

Martha was in Jane's inner circle and allowed to read an early version of what became *Pride and Prejudice*. Jane joked to Cassandra, 'I would not let Martha read First Impressions again upon any account, & am very glad that I did not leave it in your power.—She is very cunning, but I see through her design;—she means to publish it from Memory, & one more perusal must enable her to do it.'[20] This playful spirit comes through in other correspondence regarding Martha, as well as feelings of heartfelt gratitude and sisterly devotion that would deepen in the years ahead.

Well-situated Ibthorpe

The relative proximity of Ibthorpe to Steventon enabled Jane and Cassandra to visit the Lloyds often. Likewise, Ibthorpe provided a handy stopover for family members en route to Kintbury or Bath. Jane exclaimed, 'I love Martha better than ever, & I mean to go & see her if I can, when she gets home.'[21] After one such stay in December 1800, Martha accompanied Jane back home to Steventon. Martha's sister Mary was already there in anticipation of their arrival. According to the family story, Mrs Austen greeted Jane and Martha at the rectory door with the announcement of Mr Austen's retirement: 'Well girls, it is all settled, we have decided to leave Steventon in such a week and go to Bath.'[22] Jane was greatly distressed. She must have imagined settling

Detail of an 1826 *County of Southampton* survey map with significant locations in Martha Lloyd's life highlighted: Ibthorpe, Dean[e], Steventon, Winchester and Chawton.

in at the parsonage but instead was faced with the prospect of leaving her girlhood home. Surely Jane appreciated having Martha by her side for such unsettling news.

Martha stayed with Jane and her family until early January 1801. No doubt the friends had much to discuss regarding the upcoming move. During this time, Martha helped Jane sort through her father's 500-volume library in preparation for the sale.[23] Martha returned to Steventon a few weeks later and probably assisted with other tasks. In early May, just before the sale of the parsonage contents, Mr Austen departed for Bath. Mrs Austen, Cassandra and Jane left their home for the companionship of the Lloyds at Ibthorpe and awaited news of the sale.[24]

After Jane moved to Bath, Martha surely received news from her friend when the Austens stayed initially with the Leigh-Perrots then settled midsummer at 4 Sydney Place.[25] Martha's name appears several times in Jane's letters to Cassandra, especially in reference to garment styles and when Cassandra takes on a sewing project for Martha: 'When you have made Martha's bonnet you must make her a cloak of the same sort of materials; they are very much worn here, in different forms—many of them just like her black silk spencer, with a trimming round the armholes instead of the Sleeves.'[26]

In June 1804, Martha's uncle John Craven died suddenly of apoplexy. By this time, Mrs Lloyd had survived a similar stroke, but was left impaired in mind and body. Martha and her sisters shielded their mother from their uncle's death, fearful that it might bring on another stroke. Eventually Mrs Lloyd became cognizant of her brother's absence, even though Martha and her sisters refrained from wearing mourning clothes in the presence of their mother. Over the next several months, Martha's mother suffered repeated paralytic seizures that left her increasingly disabled and in even greater need of Martha's care.[27]

We have no surviving correspondence between Martha and Jane from January 1805 when Mr Austen died in Bath, but Martha certainly offered consolation and sympathy to her dear friend. Martha had experienced her own father's death—and at an age similar to Jane. Within three short months of her friend's loss, Martha's mother lay dying. Cassandra came to Ibthorpe to help Martha nurse the failing Mrs Lloyd.[28] Jane assured her sister, 'As a companion You will be all that Martha can be supposed to want; & in that light, under those circumstances your visit will indeed have been well-timed, & your presence & support have the utmost value.'[29] Jane knew with certainty that Cassandra's presence would be a balm to Martha even at her mother's deathbed.

When Martha had a frustrating delay with her mourning clothes, Jane and Mrs Austen collaborated to write verses to cheer their friend:

Lines supposed to have been sent to an uncivil Dress maker—

Miss Lloyd has now sent to Miss Green,
As, on opening the box, may be seen,
Some yards of a Black Ploughman's Gauze,
To be made up directly, because
Miss Lloyd must in mourning appear—
For the death of a Relative dear—
Miss Lloyd must expect to receive
This license to mourn & to grieve,
Complete, er'e the end of the week—
It is better to write than to speak—
  Jane Austen

Miss Green's reply
by Mrs Austen

I've often made clothes
For those who wrote prose,
But 'tis the first time
I've had orders in rhyme—.
Depend on't, fair Maid,
You shall be obeyed;
Your garment of black
Shall sit close to your back,

And in every part
I'll exert all my art;
It shall be the neatest,
And eke the completest
That ever was seen—
Or my name is not Green![30]

One week after the death of Mrs Lloyd, Jane informed her brother
Frank that his sisters and mother planned to join with Martha and
form one household. Jane assumed that her family would anticipate this
'intended Partnership' with Martha. 'None of <u>our</u> nearest connections
I think will be unprepared for it; & I do not know how to suppose that
Martha's have not foreseen it.'[31] Jane wrote with confidence that both
sides of the family would see this shared home as a foregone conclusion.
Perhaps the natural closeness between the women made it obvious that
the widow Austen and spinsters Jane, Cassandra and Martha would
live together going forward. Clearly these women had strong economic
motivation for banding together. Although Georgian society was patri-
archal, there were numerous examples of female households formed by
either circumstance or choice. Martha lived in a female household after
the death of her father, as did Jane. Examples of female households in
Jane Austen's works cross various economic levels, from the poor Bates
women in *Emma* to the dispossessed Dashwoods in *Sense and Sensibility*
and the aristocratic de Bourghs in *Pride and Prejudice*.

Martha was probably very relieved and grateful that Cassandra
stayed at Ibthorpe through early May to help with the sale of the estate.
With Martha's younger sisters married and settled, Mrs Lloyd left her
eldest daughter with all the ready cash and the contents of the house
while the lease on Ibthorpe was being settled. The Lloyd estate as a
whole was divided equally among the three daughters.[32] There is no
indication that the Lloyd sisters were anything but grateful for their
inheritance. Certainly it would not be in Martha's nature to contest her
mother's will or strive to gain financially from her sisters.

In September, the Austen women and Martha took a refreshing holiday to Worthing, joined for a time by brother Edward with his family from Godmersham. The following spring, Mrs Austen searched Bath for affordable lodgings—undoubtedly with space for Martha in mind. We know that Martha was currently lodging elsewhere in Bath because Jane visited her on 9 April 1806 to check on her recovery from a recent and unspecified accident. Jane found her friend fairly well but rather tired.[33] This is one of the few reports of Martha being indisposed. Overall, she must have enjoyed remarkably good health, especially compared with Mrs Austen, who was frequently ill. Jane's letters mention Martha suffering only minor maladies at various times such as a cold, aches or chilblains.

In July 1806 the women left Bath for good. The Austens went to Clifton while Martha was bound for Harrogate.[34] Jane wrote an eleven-stanza poem comically rebuking Mr Best, a Lloyd family friend, for not accompanying Martha on her journey:

To Martha
Oh! Mr Best, you're very bad
And all the world shall know it;
Your base behaviour shall be sung
By me, a tuneful Poet.—

You used to go to Harrowgate
Each summer as it came,
And why I pray should you refuse
To go this year the same?—

The way's as plain, the road's as smooth,
The Posting not increased;
You're scarcely stouter than you were,
Not younger Sir at least.—

If e'er the waters were of use
Why now their use forego?
You may not live another year,
All's mortal here below.—

It is your duty Mr Best
To give your health repair.
Vain else your Richard's pills[35] will be,
And vain your Consort's care.

But yet a nobler Duty calls
You now towards the North.
Arise ennobled—as Escort
Of Martha Lloyd stand forth.

She wants your aid—she honours you
With a distinguish'd call.
Stand forth to be the friend of her
Who is the friend of all.—

Take her, & wonder at your luck,
In having such a Trust.
Her converse sensible & sweet
Will banish heat & dust.—

So short she'll make the journey seem
You'll bid the Chaise stand still.
T'will be like driving at full speed
From Newb'ry to Speen Hill.—

Convey her safe to Morton's wife[36]
And I'll forget the past,
And write some verses in your praise
As finely & as fast.

But if you still refuse to go
I'll never let you rest,
But haunt you with reproachful song,
Oh! wicked Mr Best!—

J.A.
Clifton 1806[37]

Mr Best lived in Newbury and would have known its proximity to Speen Hill. Jane employed hyperbole to describe Martha's company

14

as so delightful that it would make the 236-mile journey from Bath to Harrogate pass as quickly as the 2-mile jaunt from Newbury to Speen Hill. Around this time, Jane also wrote a poem for her brother Frank. The amusing five-stanza verse imagined Frank and his bride Mary travelling on their honeymoon to Godmersham, the Kent home of brother Edward. These poetic examples show Jane affectionately using her writing talents for a beloved brother and a cherished friend.

Life in Southampton

Over the course of the next few months, Martha's prospects improved considerably. As intended, Jane's sailor brother Frank married Mary Gibson of Ramsgate on 24 July 1806. By October, Martha was invited to share a Southampton home with the newlyweds, Jane, Cassandra and their mother. Understandably, Frank wanted his new bride to have company while he was away at sea.[38]

The party stayed in temporary lodgings in Southampton until March 1807 while Frank arranged for the Castle Square house and gardens to be improved. Some of this time, Martha travelled to see relatives and friends, including the Debary family. Revd Peter Debary was newly appointed rector at Eversley. Jane wrote to Cassandra: 'I cannot help thinking she will marry Peter Debary.'[39] But Martha's own correspondence revealed otherwise, as Jane reported: 'This post has brought me Martha's own assurance of her coming on tuesday even[g] ... she does not own herself in any danger of being tempted back again however, & as she signs her maiden name we are at least to suppose her not married yet.'[40] It is hard to tell if the Austen sisters were simply amusing themselves with a romantic attachment for Martha, or if Martha herself had designs on a union with Peter Debary. What we can tell is that Martha's future happiness was once again discussed between Jane and Cassandra.

When Martha moved in with the Austens, it is quite possible that she contributed financially to the Castle Square home—especially

Detail of *Southampton by Moonlight* by Sebastian Pether, 1820. Martha Lloyd lived in Capt. Francis Austen's Castle Square home, depicted directly above the larger arch in the sea wall.

considering her recent inheritance from her mother. Martha's contribution would have been welcomed by Frank, who had not received his due from commanding HMS *Canopus*. 'Because of the loss through storm damage of the ship's books … Captain Frank Austen had as yet received no pay for his period of command of that vessel—March 1805 to June 1806—nor any subsequent half-pay. His claim was not settled until January 1808.'[41] It would certainly be in character for Martha to help if she could.

Martha enjoyed her years living with the Austens at Castle Square. She had come from a family of six and, except for occasional visits, spent the last eight years living with her mother in limited company at Ibthorpe. The constant companions and frequent visitors to the commodious old house at Castle Square made an excellent home for the affable Martha. As Jane wrote to Cassandra at Godmersham, 'Martha thanks you for your message, & desires you may be told with her best

Love that your wishes are answered & that she is full of peace & comfort here.'[42] Martha's room was outfitted as smartly as the other bedrooms. 'There will be green baize enough for Martha's room & ours … Mary is to have a piece of Carpeting for the same purpose; my mother says she does not want any; & it may certainly be better done without in her room than in Martha's & ours.'[43] Clearly Mrs Austen would not take the luxury of carpet away from Martha any sooner than she would from her own daughters.

When in town, Martha could walk with Jane along the ancient city walls and feel refreshed by the sea breezes. She could journey to Winchester, walk about the town with the three college boys (nephew Fulwar-William Fowle and Jane's nephews Edward and George Austen), then treat them with a visit to the pastry cook. When she returned from travel, Martha was greeted by her loving and considerate extended family. In expectation of Martha's arrival, Jane wrote to Cassandra, 'You know of course that Martha comes today; yesterday brought us notice of it, & the Spruce Beer is brewed in consequence.'[44] The Castle Square cellar was probably spacious, because Jane also made reference to the making of orange wine. This indicates that the cellar had ample storage for casks of both wine and beer. The kitchen had room enough for Mrs Austen to cure six hams for Frank's voyages. The garden was the envy of their neighbours, producing gooseberries, raspberries and even currants well beyond the usual season because the old city wall ran along one side and provided shelter from cold winds.[45] The benefits of the Castle Square cellar, kitchen and garden dovetailed nicely with Martha's cookery interests. In this home, Martha was once again surrounded by people she loved and activities she enjoyed.

In October 1808, family tragedy shattered the tranquillity at Castle Square. Jane's brother Edward's wife Elizabeth died a fortnight after the birth of their eleventh child. Cassandra was with Edward's family at Godmersham when Jane wrote, 'With what true sympathy our feelings are shared by Martha, you need not be told;—she is the friend & Sister

17

under every circumstance.[46] Jane wrote with complete confidence that Cassandra would understand the full measure of Martha's sympathy. Jane's words revealed the depth of the relationship—that both she and Cassandra felt a connection to Martha that compared with their own family bond. No other friend garnered such praise or enjoyed such intimacy with the Austen sisters as Martha Lloyd.

Very shortly after Elizabeth Austen's death, Edward offered his mother the choice of two homes, one near each of his estates in Hampshire and in Kent. Mrs Austen selected Chawton Cottage in Hampshire, probably because she was already considering a move to Alton, the market town near Chawton village.[47] The Austen women prepared to move—and naturally Martha was included in their plans. Happily, Mrs Austen picked the location Martha would have chosen for herself—one that placed her close to the company she kept while living at Deane and Ibthorpe; one that shortened the journeys to her sisters at Steventon and Kintbury.

Before leaving town, Jane hoped her visiting brother (presumably James) would take the ladies out one night to see a play. 'Martha ought to see the inside of the Theatre once while she lives in Southampton.'[48] Jane and Martha took in a ball at the Dolphin Hotel, in the same room where they danced fifteen years before.[49] Jane made every effort to enjoy the delights of Southampton before their departure, and she saw that Martha received her share of the fun.

The Austens hosted evening parties at Castle Square to take leave of their local acquaintances. At one such gathering, Jane observed Miss Jane Murden 'sitting very ungracious & very silent with us from 7 o'clock, till after 11'. But the next evening, 'Miss Murden was quite a different creature … oweing to her having with Martha's help found a situation in the morn^g which bids very fair for comfort.' Miss Murden was a relation of Martha's, who had recently lost her mother, Christiana Fowle Murden, and was uncertain of her future. The empathetic Martha, having lost her own mother three years prior, arranged for

Miss Murden to lodge with the local apothecary's widow, Mrs Hookey. Jane added, 'I was truely glad to see her comfortable in Mind and spirits;—at her age perhaps one may be as friendless oneself, & in similar circumstances quite as captious.'[50] Miss Murden died in 1820 and returned Martha's kindness with a legacy.[51] Even though years may have passed, people remembered Martha's goodness.

At Chawton Cottage

The next months were filled with excitement as the women anticipated their new home. The cottage had six bedchambers, a good kitchen, ample cellar, garrets for storage, a bakehouse, garden and orchard. There was space to keep chickens and for Cassandra to keep bees as she did at Steventon. The benefits of Chawton Cottage and its available land promised the Austen women the most productive food environment since their years at Steventon—and Martha must have looked forward to focusing on her cookery interests.

From Jane's letters, we know that Martha's bedroom was large. When travelling, Martha offered the use of her room to Jane's niece. 'Lizzy was much obliged to you for your message, but she had the little room. Her Father having his choice & being used to a very large Bed-chamber at home, would of course prefer the ample space of Yours.'[52] Currently, staff members of Jane Austen's House have offices in the space they believe was Martha's bedroom, directly above the kitchen in the long wing of the L-shaped house. We don't know if this location was selected to give Martha a measure of privacy or perhaps some additional warmth in the winter. If the back stairs can be confirmed as dating to this period, they would have provided Martha with easy access to the kitchen and a way to monitor the cook's work.

The July 1809 move into Chawton Cottage signalled a change in domestic responsibilities. Mrs Austen, at nearly 70 years of age, decided to focus on her gardening and patchwork, leaving the general household management to Cassandra and Martha. Jane made the family breakfast

Chawton Cottage, known today as Jane Austen's House, where the Austen women and Martha Lloyd moved in 1809. Martha's bedroom was upstairs to the left, above the kitchen.

and kept an eye on supplies of sugar, tea and wine. This arrangement gave Jane plenty of time for her writing, an activity the entire household was certainly aware of. Martha must have known that Jane scrambled to hide her small sheets of paper whenever visitors or servants pushed the creaky swinging door. Surely Martha enjoyed listening as Jane read her work aloud—just as she did with her early writing at Steventon. Martha dutifully kept Jane's authorship a secret, but no doubt felt a measure of pride as the writer's identity became known throughout the neighbourhood. It is only from Jane's letter to Martha that we have the purchase details of *Pride and Prejudice* prior to its publication.

> P. & P. is sold.—Egerton gives £110 for it.—I would rather have had £150, but we could not both be pleased, & I am not at all surprised that he should not chuse to hazard so much.—Its' being sold will I hope be a great saving of Trouble to Henry, & therefore must be welcome to me.—The Money is to be paid at the end of the twelvemonth.[53]

Years later, Jane's correspondence revealed that she expected Martha to be one of her confidantes regarding the royal request to dedicate *Emma* to H.R.H. The Prince Regent. Jane wrote to Cassandra, 'I hope you have told Martha of my first resolution of letting nobody know that I might dedicate &c—for fear of being obliged to do it.'[54] Clearly Jane trusted her secret to be as safe with Martha as it was with Cassandra.

In and nearby Chawton, Martha dined with many of the same families as the Austens: Bigg, Chute, Digweed, Lefroy, Papillon, Terry and others. Whenever Edward and his family were in residence at the Great House, Martha attended many family dinners with Jane or Cassandra—and reciprocated when Edward's family dined at the cottage. The same was true when Frank took up residence at the Great House for a period of two years. Martha was also welcome to visit Chawton House on her own. In July of 1813, Jane's niece Fanny Knight wrote, 'Miss Lloyd came in the morng. to hear me play.'[55] We can assume that Fanny was playing the piano at the time, because a year later Jane wrote that Martha was pleased to hear of Fanny learning the harp.[56] Fanny must have valued Martha's good opinion and appreciated whenever Aunt Jane conveyed it.

Chawton House in 2008, once the home of Jane Austen's brother Edward Austen Knight, where Martha Lloyd enjoyed tea, family meals and walks around the grounds.

On a trip to London, Martha purchased a Wedgwood breakfast set as a gift for Mrs Austen. Jane anticipated the delivery: 'I hope it will come by the Waggon tomorrow; it is certainly what we want, & I long to know what it is like; & as I am sure Martha has great pleasure in making the present, I will not have any regret.'[57] This generosity was typical of Martha, and the Austen sisters enabled their friend in such acts: 'You have sometimes expressed a wish of making Miss Benn some present,—Cassandra & I think that something of the Shawl kind to wear over her Shoulders within doors in very cold weather might be useful, but it must not be very handsome or she would not use it.'[58] There is a similar account of Martha sending a gift parcel for Jane to present to Mrs Digweed. 'Martha may guess how full of wonder & gratitude she was.'[59] These acts of kindness were enjoyed not only by the recipients, but by the Austens who played a part in them.

Over the years, Martha spent considerable time at the cottage with Mrs Austen, enabling both Jane and Cassandra to be away. Jane's letters show that she, Martha and Cassandra coordinated their travel plans in accordance with the unwritten family rule that Mrs Austen never stay alone at the cottage.[60] Jane wrote about keeping her absence brief: 'my Mother would be quite disappointed by my exceeding the fortnight which I now talk of as the outside;—at least we could not both remain longer away comfortably.—The middle of July is Martha's time, as far as she has any time.'[61] Martha shared equally in the task of caring for Mrs Austen, and Jane and Cassandra also benefited from Martha's sense of responsibility and duty.

By September of 1816 Jane was more frequently ill. Martha attended both Mrs Austen and Jane while Cassandra escorted Martha's sister Mary to the spa town of Cheltenham in Gloucestershire for treatment.[62] The same was true when Cassandra travelled to Berkshire after the death of her uncle, Mr James Leigh-Perrot, at his Scarlets home at Hare Hatch.[63] By May, Jane was slipping away. In a letter to friend Anne Sharpe, Jane expressed gratitude for her caregivers: 'In short, if I live to be an old Woman I must expect to wish I had died now, blessed in the tenderness of such a Family, & before I had survived either them or their affection.'[64] Surely Martha was included in this praise. Two days later, when Cassandra accompanied Jane to Winchester for more extensive care, Martha remained in Chawton with Mrs Austen. We can imagine the two women consoling each other when news of Jane's death reached the cottage at noon on 18 July.

Life beyond Jane

Very shortly after Jane's death, Mrs Austen felt compelled to make her last will. Her sons Frank and Henry served as witnesses, along with Martha Lloyd. Mrs Austen, Cassandra and Martha continued to live together at the cottage until Mrs Austen died in 1827.

Since about 1820 Frank and his family had been living in Gosport on the south coast, not far from Portsmouth. Frank's eldest daughter Mary-Jane had been managing the household from the time of her mother's death in 1823. But after five years in this role, Mary-Jane married Lieut. George Maitland Purvis on 10 June 1828. Frank would later describe this period in his memoir. Writing in the third person, he recalled, 'Finding his situation very lonely after his daughter's marriage, he selected as his second wife a lady he had long and intimately known and considered almost a sister, Miss Martha Lloyd.'[65] Frank did not suffer loneliness for long; he and Martha announced their engagement the following month.[66]

On 24 July 1828 Francis William Austen (aged 54) and Martha Lloyd (aged 62) were married in Winchester.[67] The couple selected Frank and Mary's wedding anniversary as the day for their own union. Surely this gesture reflected the fondness Martha felt towards Frank's first wife. Martha, the mature former spinster, became a bride and stepped into Frank's family of ten children ranging in ages from 7 to 21.

Martha already fitted naturally within the Austen family, but Frank's aunt Mrs James Leigh-Perrot soon revealed her displeasure with his choice. Years before, when Frank was married to Mary Gibson, he hoped to inherit the Leigh-Perrot estate of Scarlets. This expectation may have inspired the name of Frank and Mary's last-born son Cholmeley—his aunt and godmother's maiden name. Sadly, Cholmeley's birth resulted in the death of Frank's first wife and the poor child lived for only six months.

Perhaps second-wife Martha was simply not the mistress Mrs Leigh-Perrot imagined for Scarlets, because Frank's wealthy aunt turned her favour elsewhere. When her great-nephew James-Edward became engaged to the elegant Emma Smith of Tring Park, Mrs Leigh-Perrot doubled his annual allowance from £300 to £600 and provided his mother with £100 per year for his expenses.[68] James-Edward later wrote to his fiancée, 'Marriage which has sunk my uncle has raised me in her favour.'[69] Apparently, this is the only negative consequence of Frank and Martha's union, but it was a costly one.

Martha probably sensed Mrs Leigh-Perrot's dislike, and Frank must have shared both his expectation and fear of disappointment with his new wife. But not a hint of bitterness was directed to James-Edward when Martha conveyed their warm congratulations from Gosport:

> Government House
> Sep^{tr} 30th
>
> My dear Edward
> Your very interesting communication reached me this Morn$_g$. & I feel obliged to you for its detailed account, & bestowing so much of your precious time upon me when it must be so valuable to another—Your Uncle & I beg you to accept our warm & sincere congratulations on your 'opening prospect of wedded happiness' & I am anxious that you should receive them whilst at Tring Park, that you may communicate them to, & share them with the object of your affection, to whom also we beg you will endeavor to make them acceptable—The name of Miss Emma Smith, has long been familiar to me, & whilst I cannot but think you have been most fortunate in gaining the affections of such a Woman as I have

always believed her to be, it may be allowed to an affectionate Aunt's partiallity, to believe that she has also a share in the good fortune in becoming the beloved Wife, of a Man of good principle, good sense, & good temper, & one who ~~will~~ I verily think will make her a good husband. May you both be as happy as I wish you, & as such a state is capable of making you!—you yourselves cannot wish for more; & may that God who gives or witholds his blessings, pour them plentifully upon you!—We rejoice greatly in Mrs. Leigh Perrots liberallity to you, & that it should be extended to your Mother & Sister—She seldom does things by halves, & in this instance has acted in character—With respect to your seeing us at Newtown, it is I must not say <u>I fear</u> quite out of the question, for we cannot be there this year, & I must not wish you to remain to another. I trust however we shall meet again, if not before you have a Bride to present to me; afterwards—In the meantime you can tell her, what it is a matter of form to subscribe myself, that I am my

    dear Edward

      your truly affectionate

        Aunt

        Martha Austen[70]

In October, Mrs Leigh-Perrot wrote to James-Edward of her intention to bequeath Scarlets to him. She reasoned that he and Emma would reside on the estate, but Frank and Martha might not.[71] Of course, James-Edward dashed off a note to Emma, sharing the good news.

The young couple were married on 16 December, Jane Austen's birthday. Within a week, Mrs Leigh-Perrot wrote her congratulations to the newlyweds. By this time, Frank had sent his aunt what must have been a very pointed letter, because she burned it and refused to respond.[72] By the following September, James-Edward and Emma welcomed their first child. They named the boy Cholmeley and asked Mrs Leigh-Perrot to be his godmother.[73] We don't know what Frank and Martha thought as they watched part of the Austen family history being repeated.

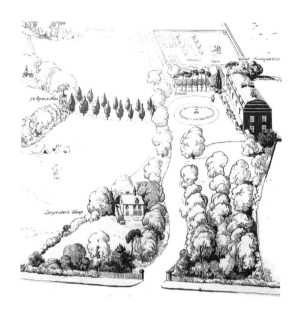

Martha and Capt. Francis Austen's home Portsdown Lodge, later the site of Boundary Oak School, 1921–60. Detail of *c.*1930 illustration currently hanging in the headmaster's study, artist unknown.

The following spring was a challenging one for Frank and Martha. Frank's third daughter Elizabeth died on 22 May 1830. She was just 13 years old. A few weeks later, he again quarrelled with Aunt Leigh-Perrot. In lieu of leaving him Scarlets, she gave Frank a total of £11,600 and permanently distanced herself from him.[74]

These events, however unhappy, signalled some positive changes for Frank and Martha. In what appears to be in consequence of his aunt's settlement, Frank purchased Portsdown Lodge near Portsmouth. A later advertisement for the house described it as having 'four living rooms and fourteen bedrooms, plus servants' quarters, farm buildings and twenty-five acres of rich pasture land'.[75] Later pencil sketches by Frank's daughter Catherine show the property with a cricket field and archery equipment.[76] Shortly after he purchased the house, Frank was promoted to rear admiral.[77] Life was definitely improving for Frank and Martha.

By all accounts, Frank and Martha had a happy and lively home. Frank's sister Cassandra and Martha's sister Mary visited often and for weeks at a time. Frank's three daughters still at home, Cassandra-Eliza,

Catherine-Anne and Frances-Sophia, would hear their aunt and step-mother reminisce about Aunt Jane. Cassandra read aloud from the novels and unpublished fragments known to us as *The Watsons* and *Sanditon*. Years later, Catherine wrote her own ending to *The Watsons* and published it as *The Younger Sister* in 1850.[78] James-Edward was also quite welcome in his uncle's home.

On more than one occasion, Frank attempted to see his estranged Aunt Leigh-Perrot, but each time she declined. When she wrote to James-Edward, she was curious about Martha's appearance, but never renewed any connection with Frank.[79] Sadly, Frank did not return to Scarlets until after Mrs Leigh-Perrot's death in November of 1836 when he and brothers Henry and Charles gathered with the other mourners for her funeral.[80]

In February of the following year, Frank was made Knight Commander of the Bath. He and Martha became Admiral Sir Francis and Lady Austen. Cassandra congratulated Martha with the gift of Jane's copy of *Camilla*.[81] In 1838 Frank received his commission of Vice Admiral of the Blue.[82] The national census of 1841 recorded that daughters Cassandra, Catherine and Frances were still living at home with Frank and Martha, along with eight servants. Martha's life had changed dramatically since her spinsterhood, but even through her last years we can see that her concern for others remained constant.

On an August morning in 1842 Catherine married promising barrister John Hubback, with her cousin James-Edward performing the ceremony. Frank's sister Cassandra recounted the festivities in a letter to niece Anna Lefroy. She described the wedding party's attire, how movingly James-Edward read the service, plus details of the pretty luncheon lovingly arranged by Martha. 'Nothing could have been more kindly & considerately done than every thing has been done by your Aunt. I am afraid she has been exerting herself too much for her own health, which certainly is not in its best state—but perhaps the weather may have had something to do with it.'[83]

Martha's apparent fatigue had little to do with the thunderstorm that began soon after the wedding couple left. She had an underlying condition, recorded on her death certificate as 'General debility & decay of the digestive powers'. She died on 24 January 1843 in the presence of her beloved Frank. Cassandra arrived to find her brother deeply afflicted. He was more composed the next day at Martha's funeral and as she was buried in the churchyard of St Peter & St Paul in Wymering, Hampshire.[84] Her epitaph reads:

Here rest the remains of
MARTHA
the wife of Vice Admiral Sir Francis Austen K.C.B.
Beloved esteemed and respected by all who knew her
she closed her life of Christian benevolence and practical piety
deeply lamented by her surviving relations
Jan. 24th 1843
Aged 77 years
Blessed are the pure who die in the Lord.

The day after the funeral, Cassandra wrote to Anna Lefroy:

Your dear Aunt was of so much importance in this House & so unremitting in her endeavours to make every individual comfortable, that she must be missed by all. For myself, I can think of no residence during the last fifty years where I have not been in the habit of frequently seeing her, but in this place more especially do I miss her, for here I have never till now been without her. She has been to me an affecte., a tried & faithful friend for at least half a century, & we have been connected by so many interesting ties, that she must retain a prominent place in my thoughts during the short remainder of my Life.[85]

At Martha's request, her amethyst brooch was given to James-Edward's wife Emma, and her garnet hoop ring was given to Cassandra, who later bequeathed it to niece Caroline Austen.[86] Cassandra died two years later at Portsdown Lodge after suffering a stroke. She had come

The grave of Martha Austen (née Lloyd) as seen today in the churchyard of St Peter & St Paul in Wymering, Hampshire.

to see Frank before he set sail on his final commission.[87] Cassandra was buried in Chawton alongside her mother. Frank's second daughter, Cassandra-Eliza, died unmarried on 6 May 1849, aged 35. She was buried at Wymering beside Martha, suggesting the closeness of their relationship.

Frank decided to make his own will in October 1857. In it he fulfilled promises to Martha by distributing various small legacies. For himself, he requested a quiet funeral and to be buried in the Wymering churchyard with Martha.[88] On 27 April 1863 Francis William Austen was promoted to Admiral of the Fleet, the highest rank of the Royal Navy. He died on 10 August 1865 at the age of 91. His grave marker bears a simple cross accompanied by his and Martha's initials and respective years of death. In his old age, Frank wrote of Martha, 'Joined to the possession of much good sense, she possessed the blessings of a sweet temper, amiable disposition and what is of far greater importance a mind deeply impressed with the truth of Christianity.'[89]

Martha myths

As of the publication of this work, no detailed physical description or image of Martha Lloyd has been discovered. There are two scant references in Jane's letters: 'Martha looks very well, & wants me to find out that she grows fat'[90] and 'I hope the Shoes will fit; Martha & I both tried them on.'[91] Regarding Martha's figure, Jane could not agree with her friend. Perhaps Martha desired a more shapely form in keeping with the current standards of beauty. From the shoe reference, all we can deduce is that Martha and Jane may have been similar in height. The lack of physical detail adds to the mystery of Martha.

For many years, an early photograph of a kindly looking woman with a dog on her lap was said to be Martha. Thought to be a daguerreotype and thus contemporary to Martha, the image was acquired by the Jane Austen Society. In 1978, George Holbert Tucker examined the image under magnification and thought he saw a cross around the neck of the subject. He determined that the cross was fashioned from five oval topaz stones and was identical to the one given Jane by her brother Charles in 1801. Tucker hypothesized that the portrait showed Jane's cross being worn by Martha Lloyd.[92] This misidentification fuelled the myth that after Jane's death Cassandra gave the cross as a memento to Martha, who supposedly wore it for the rest of her life.

In 2015 a visitor to Jane Austen's House suspected that the image was not actually a daguerreotype. Shortly afterwards, colleagues from the Victoria and Albert Museum identified the portrait as an ambrotype, a photographic technique invented after Martha's death. To further disprove Tucker's hypothesis, the topaz crosses given to Jane and Cassandra were passed through descendants of Charles Austen, not those of Frank.[93]

Today we know that the woman in the old photograph is not Martha, and that Cassandra never gave Jane's topaz cross to Martha as a keepsake. Although facts have the power to dispel myths, the close bond between Martha, Jane and Cassandra made it plausible for these stories to stand as truth for nearly forty years.

Martha's household book in historical context

In the eighteenth century a lady's household book was an essential tool for managing her home. Whether she lived on a large estate or dwelled in a modest cottage, her handwritten collection of culinary recipes, household preparations and medicinal cures created a ready resource for daily living. Although the need for a household book was universal, the content and format varied considerably. Martha Lloyd's collection was specific to her own experience—as each woman's was to her individual situation. But certain features are common to many household books from this period, so it is helpful to look at Martha's work in a broader context before we explore its unique details.

The product of a female network

The creation of a household book was largely a female endeavour. Although men such as Parson James Woodforde (1740–1803) of Norfolk certainly recorded food, livestock and remedy information,[1] they did so primarily as diarists. Women prepared for their families' needs. Meals must be made, beer must be brewed and anyone or anything that drew breath may eventually need a cure. It was a woman's responsibility to be ready for any household requirement, and that preparation began at her mother's side and continued through her adult life.

Household wisdom was handed down from generation to generation, and the household book was the standard repository for indispensable and retrievable information. It is touching to see contributions credited to mothers, grandmothers, aunts and hosts of other relatives and friends who formed a predominantly female network for domestic information. When Elizabeth Ambler (1712–1766) penned entries at her family home in Berkshire, she could not have imagined that her household book would be handed down through five generations of female descendants over nearly three hundred years.[2] Similarly, Martha recorded contributions from her own female network, which included her mother Martha Lloyd (née Craven), her sister Eliza Fowle (née Lloyd) and her aunt Jane Fowle (née Craven).

Early sources

The household book evolved from its late Middle English definition as a place for recording household affairs and accounts. Gervase Markham probably provided content for household books with *The English Huswife*, first published in 1615. After a brief preface extolling 'The inward and outward vertues which ought to be in a complete woman', Markham offered 128 pages on 'Physicke, Cookery, Banqueting-stuffe, Distillation, Perfumes, Wooll, Hemp, Flax, Dayries, Brewing, Baking, and all other things belonging to an Houshould.'[3] His book was popular throughout the seventeenth century and remained in print for nearly seventy years.

Other writers loosely followed Markham's lead. At the beginning of the eighteenth century, *The Whole Duty of a Woman* offered four full chapters of spiritual and temporal guidance, followed by seven chapters on remedies, cookery, confectionery and 'artificial embellishments' or cosmetics.[4] When Eliza Smith wrote *The Compleat Housewife* in 1727 she skipped the lofty female virtues and added seasonal bills of fare and marketing advice to her cookery and medicinal content. In 1747 Hannah Glasse produced her landmark book *The Art of Cookery Made Plain and Easy*, focusing entirely on food preparation and preserving. Her popular cookbook was published well into the nineteenth century. During this

FRONTISPIECE.

The Fair, who's Wise and oft consults our Book,
And thence directions gives her Prudent Cook;
With Choicest Viands, has her Table Crown'd,
And Health, with Frugal Elegance is found.

Frances E. Downs

THE
ART of COOKERY,
MADE
PLAIN and EASY;

Which far exceeds any Thing of the Kind yet published,

CONTAINING

I. How to Roaſt and Boil to Perfec-
tion every Thing neceſſary to be
ſent up to Table.
II. Of Made Diſhes.
III. How expenſive a French Cook's
Sauce is.
IV. To make a Number of pretty little
Diſhes for a Supper or Side-diſh, and
little Corner diſhes for a great Table.
V. To dreſs Fiſh.
VI. Of Soups and Broths.
VII. Of Puddings.
VIII. Of Pies.
IX. For a Lent Dinner; a number of
good Diſhes, which you may make
Uſe of at any other Time.
X. Directions to prepare proper Food
for the Sick.
XI. For Captains of Ships; how to
make all uſeful Things for a Voy-
age; and ſetting out a Table on
board a Ship.

XII. Of Hogs Puddings, Sauſages,
&c.
XIII. To pot and make Hams, &c.
XIV. Of Pickling.
XV. Of making Cakes, &c.
XVI. Of Cheeſecakes, Creams, Jel-
lies, Whip-Syllabubs, &c.
XVII. Of made Wines, Brewing,
French Bread, Muffins, &c.
XVIII. Jarring Cherries and Preſerves,
&c.
XIX. To make Anchovies, Vermicella,
Catchup, Vinegar, and to keep Ar-
tichokes, French Beans, &c.
XX. Of Diſtilling.
XXI. How to Market; the Seaſon of
the Year for Butchers Meat, Poultry,
Fiſh, Herbs, Roots, and Fruit.
XXII. A certain cure for the Bite of a
Mad Dog. By Dr. Mead.
XXIII. A Receipt to keep clear from
Buggs.

To which are added,

One hundred and fifty New and uſeful RECEIPTS,

And a COPIOUS INDEX.

By a LADY.

A NEW EDITION.
WITH

The ORDER of a MODERN BILL of FARE, for each Month, and
the Manner the Diſhes are to be placed upon the Table.

LONDON:

Printed for a Company of Bookſellers, and ſold by L. WANGFORD, in
Fleet-Street, and all other Bookſellers in Great Britain and Ireland.

☞ Be careful to obſerve (Mrs. GLASS being dead) that the Genuine Edition
of her Art of Cookery is thus ſigned, by

W. Wangford.

The frontispiece of *The Art of Cookery Made Plain and Easy* by Hannah Glasse, c.1775,
shows a Georgian lady copying out recipes for her cook to prepare.

period, the subjects of cookery and remedies seemed to part ways with the topic of female conduct. In 1805 the conduct book[5] recommended to Jane Austen by her sister Cassandra addressed women's education, matrimony and domestic felicity, but provided no recipes or cures.

Tailoring the contents

As families and situations varied, so did the contents of women's household books. Before she married at the relatively late age of 34, Elizabeth Ambler had the responsibility of caring for her epileptic brother and ailing father. As a result, her book contains primarily Georgian remedies and cures with only an occasional culinary recipe. Elizabeth's 'Physick Book' reflects her focus on family health, revealing nothing of the comfortable surroundings and beautiful homes in which she lived.[6]

In complete contrast, Susanna Whatman's household book is all about the maintenance and preservation of her stately home. This is not to say that Susanna was materialistic or proud, but that her husband's status set a high bar for hospitality. In 1776 Susanna Bosanquet married James Whatman, an eminent English papermaker who had been named High Sheriff of Kent in 1766. His wealth and position set certain expectations, and Susanna's job was to meet or exceed them. Her book detailed myriad duties for her many servants, from housekeeper to cook, laundry maid, chambermaid and dairymaid.[7]

About this same time in Hampshire, various ladies of the Montagu family of Beaulieu were adding to their own collection.[8] Their household book, begun in the mid-eighteenth century and continuing to the early nineteenth century, is similar in content to Martha's book. The Montagu women recorded primarily food-focused instructions and fewer household preparations and medical or veterinary cures. Comparable in size to Martha's 196-recipe collection, the Montagu collection is but half the size of the robust *Knight Family Cookbook* containing nearly four hundred recipes from Jane Austen's Hampshire and Kent connections.[9] The Montagu and Knight collections contain recipes for ices and their accompanying sauces; each book signals the presence of an icehouse and thereby the affluence of the landowner. Because Martha had no ready access to ice, her book contains no such recipes.

Copying from cookbooks

In addition to consulting her resourceful female network, a woman might copy out recipes from published cookbooks. Like other books, cookbooks were costly and the typical eighteenth-century household could not boast of having the variety of titles that ours do today. But circulating libraries like those of John Bell and John Boosey in London offered numerous works from culinary experts such as Hannah Glasse, Elizabeth Smith, Martha Bradley, Elizabeth Raffald and Charlotte Mason.[10] It was a common practice for women to copy printed recipes verbatim into their household books and in turn share those recipes with relatives and neighbours. Martha could have copied any number of recipes from cookbooks borrowed from circulating libraries. Like Jane and Cassandra Austen, Martha's sister Mary had a subscription to Mrs Martin's circulating library operating in Basingstoke from 1798 to 1800.[11]

Reading a number of household books reveals a striking similarity in the recipe language, and some of Martha's recipes mirror those found in the household books of her contemporaries. Martha's recipe 'To Make light Wigs' follows nearly word for word that of Hannah Glasse in *The Art of Cookery Made Plain and Easy*. A few trivial omissions were made, perhaps by Martha or by the woman from whom she copied. But somewhere along the way the critical last line of Glasse's recipe was left off: 'Mind to mix a quarter of a Pint of good Ale-Yeast in the Milk.'[12] Unfortunately, making the rolls directly from Martha's book would result in rather heavy instead of light wigs. Some of Martha's other entries match their printed counterparts nearly verbatim: 'To make

...ful & Spinach & beat of each a small quantity
half a spoonful of Sugar ... the Soup to be boiled
as thick as you like it and the Whole to be all
to-gether boiled up & Dished. ___

To Make light Wigs

Take a p⁴ & half of flour & half a pint of ...
Made Warm, mix these together, and ...
let it stand by the fire half an hour, then ...
half a p⁴ of Butter & half a ... Sugar
these in the paste and make it int wigs ...
little flour as posible; let the oven ...
& they will rise very ...

A batch of light wigs recreated in 2016 from *Martha Lloyd's Household Book* (see recipe above) demonstrates the use of the beehive oven at Chawton Cottage bakehouse.

Gooseberry Vinegar' follows Charlotte Mason's *The Lady's Assistant*,[13] and 'To Hash a Calves Head' follows Elizabeth Raffald's *The Experienced English Housekeeper*.[14]

In an affluent home the lady copied out recipes from her household book and handed them to her cook to take to the kitchen. Such a scene is depicted in the frontispiece illustration of Glasse's *The Art of Cookery*. We can imagine a similar scene at Godmersham involving the *Knight Family Cookbook*. Judging by its pristine pages, it seems highly unlikely that this book came anywhere near the kitchen. In vibrant contrast, Martha's book bears the marks of everyday life. Through apparent spills and the crumbling edges of well-worn pages, we get a picture of the kitchen bustling with activity.[15]

Collecting cures

Unlike their culinary counterparts, medicinal preparations appear to originate from far more varied sources. There is little similarity in the phrasing of home remedies found in the household books mentioned thus far, although some of the same key ingredients appear in similar cures. Camphor and opium were used for toothaches, magnesium sulphate and senna were common laxatives, and linseed oil was given to both people and livestock to rid them of worms. The healing powers of minerals, herbs, tree barks and resins were used to battle a barrage of complaints from fevers and whooping cough to kidney stones and consumption. Both the Ambler and Montagu collections incorporate snail water in tonics and eye rinses. Household books compiled in country settings often include 'A Cure for Mange in Horses or Dogs' and the necessary 'for the cure of the Bite of a Mad Dog', as does Martha's book. Medicinal ingredients were gathered from fields, woodlands, kitchen gardens and apothecaries, as women sought to apply household cures before calling a physician—or in lieu of one that may not have been readily available.

Writing in any blank book

There is no standard size or format for a household book. Martha's contemporary Elizabeth Curtis jotted down her Quaker family recipes in an 8 by 6 inch unruled copybook with a simple cardboard cover.[16] Elizabeth was the wife of Alton surgeon-apothecary William Curtis. She and Martha could have chatted after any of Martha's walks from Chawton Cottage into the nearby town. Both women collected recipes during roughly the same time period, Elizabeth beginning with her marriage in 1797 and continuing until her death in 1851.

Common to the household books discussed thus far is the use of a purchased blank book. An unusual exception to this is a household book from the Jervoise family of Herriard.[17] Their recipes were written in a section of an account book similar to one kept for Edward Austen's Chawton estate during the years Martha and the Austen women lived at the cottage.[18] The Jervoise descendants were tenants at Chawton and their rent payments were logged in Edward's ledger. Recipes in the Jervoise book fill the pages completely, crossing the printed columns intended for pounds, shillings and pence.

Working with period recipes

As with many handwritten documents from the Georgian period, spelling in household books was both irregular and creative—giving us 'pease' for peas, 'spinnage' for spinach, 'shellotts' for shallots and many others. Some examples appear to be phonetic spellings of words pronounced with regional accents, such as 'cullender' for colander and 'sallery' for celery. Abbreviations such as p^d for pound and q^t for quart were made with superscript while some words were simply cropped into shorter forms such as 'chopt' and 'whipt'. Inventive contractions replaced many –ed endings, specifying that ingredients be boil'd, weigh'd, blanch'd, pick'd, mix'd and butter'd.

Before the cook could make raspberry jam she would have to break off and grind up the sugar from a large loaf, as seen today at Jane Austen's House.

Inexperienced cooks likely struggled with variable quantities such as a 'bundle' of herbs, a 'lump' of sugar or 'a half-penny loaf' of bread. Perhaps there was more certainty in a 'teacup of broth', a piece of dough 'the size of a walnut' or crust rolled 'the thickness of a crown' coin. Occasionally, recipes had embedded quizzes, such as 'take eight eggs, leaving out two whites', or 'take half again as much flour'. Beware the cook with inferior mathematical skills.

Some recipes barely hint at the labour-intensive prep work required to produce a dish. To start with 'flour well dried', the cook had to place it before the fire to extract any moisture the flour had absorbed due to the weather or the cooking environment. If a recipe called for rice flour, the cook must first 'parch it before the fire, beat it in a Mortar & put it through a Lawn Sieve' or other fine-mesh strainer. Peppercorns had to be pounded and ground until fine, whole nutmeg needed to be grated, and butter was churned by the cook if the house did not have a dairymaid or idle children. When a recipe required candied orange or lemon peel, we can imagine who skinned, boiled and dried each sliver of peel. Any recipe including sugar required additional effort. A typical cone-shaped 'loaf' of sugar weighed between 11 and 13 pounds.[19] The cook used sugar nippers or a sugar hammer to break the loaf into smaller pieces or lumps. For fine granules, the cook pounded the lumps in a mortar with a pestle. For special sweets, she had to pound the granules until they became the soft powder we now purchase as confectioner's powdered sugar or icing sugar.

Many period recipes were written assuming a certain level of culinary knowledge or skill. The seasoned cook knew exactly what was meant by 'a quick oven' versus one that was merely 'not very hot'. Efficient cooks sequenced their baking to make use of the oven first at its highest heat, and then as it gradually cooled down. Thus mushrooms for drying went into a hot oven 'as soon as you have drawn your bread', and angelica for candy went in a cooler oven 'after the pies are drawn'. The phrasing implies that the ideal sequence for baking was universally understood.

Any kitchen veteran would know which tool to select when a recipe specified the use of a salamander, hair sieve or salting pan. But not every cook would fully comprehend the multi-step process behind the short phrase 'Make a puff paste'. No doubt the experienced dairymaid knew to use rennet to 'take out the whey' from quarts of cream and gallons of milk. Martha's cheese recipe never mentions the active ingredient for separating the curds from the whey. Similarly, we can only hope that a cook's intuition would tell her to bake the gingerbread and grill the toasted cheese, because these recipes do not explicitly say to do so.

All these recipe examples are from *Martha Lloyd's Household Book*. The language typifies that found in other household books of the period. A number of recipes from Martha's collection have been painstakingly modernized for *Dining with Jane Austen* (2019) and *The Jane Austen Cookbook* (2002). Culinary experts are encouraged to try their hand at new adaptations inspired by this facsimile edition and the annotated transcription provided. A word of caution to occasional cooks: recipes are presented as historical artefacts and not suggested in their present form for modern use. Many entries contain obsolete preparation and preservation methods that are best left to experienced recipe adaptors and food historians. Many original recipes, both culinary and medicinal, contain ingredients now known to be toxic and are not advised for consumption or use.

Unique details of Martha's book

In September 1953 R.W. Chapman of the Jane Austen Memorial Trust received a brief letter mentioning a rather curious artefact. Its owner described a discoloured and worn book 'which has Martha Lloyd's name inside & is inscribed "Cookery interest".' She listed a few of its 'many and varied receipts' and some specific contributors: Mrs Dundas, Lady Bridges, Mrs E. Knight and a Mr Jenkins whose entry was dated 1829. 'This is the only date but it looks to me as if it was started at a much earlier date. I wonder if at sometime you would let me know if the J.A. Society would be interested in it?'[1] The letter was written by Rosa Mary Mowll (née Spanton), the great-granddaughter of Francis Austen and granddaughter of his ninth child, Edward Thomas Austen.[2] Two days later, Chapman forwarded the letter to fellow trustee T. Edward Carpenter, enclosing a note of his own. He warned Carpenter that the book had 'no actual Austen in it—Lady (Francis) Austen hardly qualifies—it is of very little commercial value. Dark truth to acknowledge this.'[3]

Mrs Mowll failed to mention the book's 'actual Austen' contributions: Mrs Austen's 'Very good white Sauce for boil'd Carp', Captain Austen's Fish Sauce and several other Austen family recipes. The three correspondents didn't realize that the manuscript contained the lengthy verse now attributed to Mrs Austen and written specifically for Martha's book.[4]

Martha Lloyd's Household Book is covered in full sheep parchment and tooled with a double-lined border on the front and back. The condition of the book indicates that it was often consulted and well used since Martha began collecting recipes around 1796.

Mrs Mowll was persistent. She felt that Martha's book 'should be at Chawton which must be the home of all such relics'.[5] Eventually she revealed owning other 'Jane items of interest'.[6] A year later, Mowll pressed Carpenter with a veiled threat: 'I do not want to see anything further go to America, tho' of course the prices paid by Americans are tempting!'[7] Eventually, in May 1956, Mrs Mowll offered to sell Martha's cookery book for £5, a small price compared to the £70 she asked for Jane Austen's copy of her letter to Frank dated 26 July 1809.[8] In June 1956 *Martha Lloyd's Household Book* became part of the collection at Jane Austen's House,[9] where it remains on display in the cottage Martha and the Austen women shared.

This detail from *Martha Lloyd's Household Book*, c.1796, indicates that the primary focus of her collection was culinary recipes rather than those for household preparations or medicinal cures.

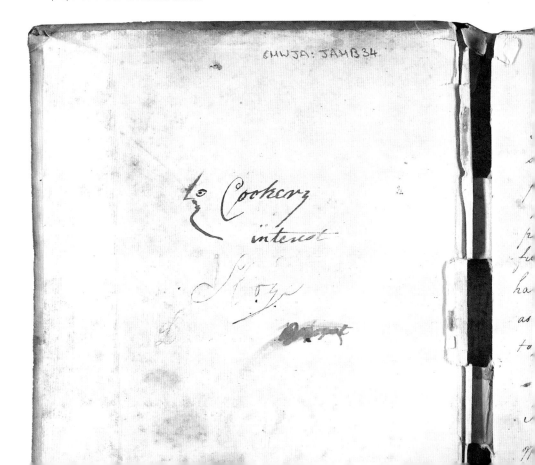

Martha at work

We may never know what prompted Martha to start her household book, but her manuscript shows her intent and work process. By inscribing 'Cookery interest' inside the front cover, she declared that her focus was culinary. She obviously numbered the first 100 pages of the book before she recorded any recipes. We can see that recipe entries she made later began to crowd the page numbers she had already placed.

Martha flipped the book upside down and back to front, and then set up tidy columns for her recipe index. Technically, when a book is printed and bound in this manner, it is called *tête–bêche*, where the beginning or head (*tête*) of the content meets the end or toe (*bêche*) of the work. Martha was clever to flip her book when starting the index because it was impossible to guess how much space the index would require. This way she could continuously add to both the front and the back of her book until the recipes and index met somewhere inside.

Physical details

Martha's book is a quarto notebook bound in full sheep parchment. The covers are tooled with a double-lined border. The outside measures 15.5 cm wide by 21.1 cm high by 2.6 cm thick. It comprises four blank signatures of varying page counts, originally totalling 126 pages. The signatures were stacked, stitched, trimmed and bound by hand.

When renowned Jane Austen scholar Deirdre Le Faye examined the book around 1990, she discovered a watermark on its inside pages. I recently identified the mark as the Maid of Dort form of the Pro Patria watermark, used primarily from 1683 to 1799.[10] Dort is the anglicized short form of Dordrecht, the oldest city in the Netherlands. The maid is seated, holding a spear with a hat on the point. Beside her is a rampant lion, brandishing a sword and clutching a bundle of arrows. The figures are located inside a palisade representing the Netherlands' fortified frontier. Although there were numerous versions of the mark, it was used primarily in Amsterdam throughout the eighteenth century when the Dutch excelled as paper manufacturers, some of which supplied paper to the British market.[11] The paper has an undated countermark with the initials GR inside a decorative circular border. No specific paper mill out of the hundreds then in existence has been associated with Martha's book.

Missing pages

The simple process of looking up each recipe from the index revealed that six pages (or three leaves) of Martha's book were missing. This unfortunate loss was discovered in 2014 when digital scans of the manuscript were referenced for the bio-cookbook *Dining with Jane Austen*. Missing pages 3–4 contained Martha's recipes for 'A Plumb Cake' and 'A White Custard'. Missing pages 23–6 included 'A Lemon Pudding', 'To make Marmalade', 'Damson Cakes', 'A fine Pancake' and 'To Make Wigs'. Versions of these recipes can be found in printed cookbooks from the period. Martha herself recorded a version entitled 'To Make light Wigs', which remains in the manuscript. In several places the original hand stitching of the signatures is visibly intact, so it is doubtful that any of the unnumbered pages also disappeared. Perhaps the missing pages simply detached as a result of normal wear and tear, especially since they appeared in the first section of recipes.

Martha's script and other handwriting

Most of the handwriting in Martha's book reflects characteristics found in her 1828 letter to nephew James-Edward. It seems needless to confirm that Martha wrote in her own book, but some household books include recipes penned through several generations. This is not the case with Martha's book, although a few of the later entries were obviously made by another hand.

Like Jane Austen, Martha frequently used an ampersand. Some of these are loosely formed and easily mistaken for the word 'or'—leaving the cook to decide if the recipe requires cloves *and* mace or the choice

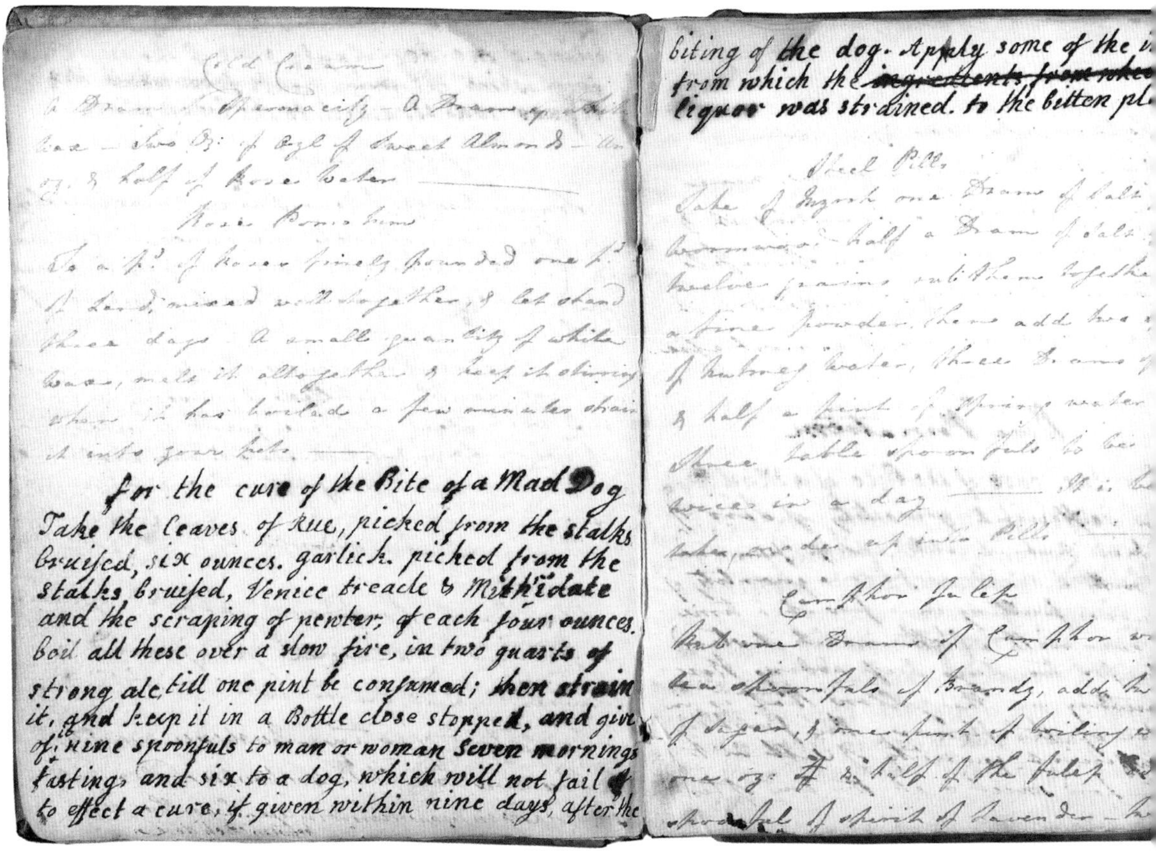
for the cure of the Bite of a Mad Dog
Take the Leaves of Rue, picked from the stalks bruised, six ounces. garlick. picked from the stalks bruised, Venice treacle & Mithridate and the scraping of pewter; of each four ounces. Boil all these over a slow fire, in two quarts of strong ale till one pint be consumed; then strain it, and keep it in a Bottle close stopped, and give of it nine spoonfuls to man or woman Seven mornings fasting, and six to a dog, which will not fail to effect a cure, if given within nine days, after the

biting of the dog. Apply some of the ingredients from which the ~~ingredients from whe~~ liquor was strained. to the bitten pl

The forced placement and different handwriting show that someone added to *Martha Lloyd's Household Book*—probably a family member and most likely after Martha died in 1843.

of cloves *or* mace. Similar quandaries arise with a number of Martha's 580 ampersands. Overall, recipes at the beginning of the book were made with more precision than those near the end.

Someone other than Martha wrote three entries: 'for the cure of the Bite of a Mad Dog', 'for a pain in the side' and 'for worms'. This person also added the note 'never Stop down your Barrel' to Martha's recipe for Gooseberry Vinegar. We know that the additions were not made by Martha's sister, Mary Austen. The handwriting does not match the recipes Mary copied into her 1836 pocketbook. The additions seem to be forced into the blank spaces Martha left. The dog bite cure appears wedged between entries for Rose Pomatum and Steel Pills. The other two cures seem crammed into the open half-page below 'A Salve for Sore eyes'. It is obvious how the writer struggled to fit the contents into the existing space.

Since we do not have handwriting samples from Martha's extended family, it is challenging to identify the mystery writer. The entries could have been made after Martha's death when Frank's daughters Cassandra-Eliza and Frances-Sophia were still living at home. Certainly they would have had access to Martha's household book.

Dating Martha's work

Although 1829 is the only date that appears in Martha's manuscript, we can use the sequence of the entries and the various contributors to approximate when she recorded in her household book. We can see that Martha copied her recipes in a continuous sequence as she collected them, so we know that the entries at the front of the book were made earlier than those at the centre. Assuming that Martha received recipes directly from her contributors and not posthumously, we can use contributor death dates to approximate the latest dates of the entries.

The contributor with the earliest death date is Lady Williams (née Jane Cooper), who lost her life in a road accident on 9 August 1798. Her 'Receipt to make Lemon Pickles' is entered on page 73 of the manuscript, so clearly Martha began making entries much earlier. Martha may have visited Lady Williams when she stayed at Steventon in 1796. So the origins of Martha Lloyd's household book certainly date to 1798 at the latest, more likely to 1796 or even slightly before.

One small notation above the recipe 'To make Hams' on page 10 indicates how late entries were made in Martha's book. The comment 'at Portsdown Lodge half the quantity of Sugar and rather more Salt than the Receipt states' must have been made after Frank Austen purchased the property around June 1830. Given the recipe sequence, their contributors and this additional notation, we know that Martha started writing in her book well before August 1798 and made additions as late as June 1830. To complete her household book, Martha made entries over the course of more than thirty years.

Contributors to Martha's book

The various contributors to Martha's book are listed below in the order they appear. Individuals who provided more than one recipe are sequenced by their first entry. The majority of Martha's contributors were known to the Austen family. There are four recipes from Mrs George Austen and two from Jane's brother Frank.

There are a few contributors for whom we have little or no information. Mrs Berry and Mrs Davison are names associated with other recipes and cures found in Mrs Ambler's household book.[12] It is likely that Martha simply received these specific recipes through sharing and did not know the contributors personally. Miss Thornhill, the contributor of 'Green Gooseberry Wine', remains a mystery. Since her contribution comes between those of Mrs Charles Fowle and Mrs Dundas, Miss Thornhill could be a family friend associated with either of these two women.

The British Library Catalogue lists publications by Dr William Turton, named specifically in 'Dr: Turton's receipt for a Cold'. No medical publications from doctors Hortigan or Molesworth could be found. These last two doctors may have been local practitioners known to Martha, or perhaps these names were simply mentioned in cures shared among family and friends.

Except for a few noted examples, all information on contributors was sourced from two publications by Deirdre Le Faye: *A Chronology of Jane Austen and Her Family: 1600–2000*[13] and *Jane Austen's Letters*.[14]

49

Mrs. Austen—Mrs George Austen was the mother of novelist Jane Austen and her siblings mentioned in this work: James, Edward, Henry, Cassandra, Francis and Charles. Although her name does not appear on one noteworthy recipe, it is believed that Mrs Austen wrote 'A receipt for a Pudding' specifically for Martha's collection. Located early in the sequence of entries, it is tempting to connect 'the vicar' of the rhymed recipe with a mysterious 'Mr W'. According to her letter from 1796, Mrs Austen believed Martha had secret intentions to marry Mr W.[15] There are several other contributions from Mrs Austen. Her recipes on manuscript page 93 were probably recorded two years before she died in 1827.

Mrs. Dundas—This is the first contributor Martha mentioned by name, although the recipe appears halfway through the culinary section of the manuscript. Mrs Ann Dundas (née Whitley) was the wife of Berkshire MP Charles Dundas and heiress of Barton Court, Kintbury. She was a friend of Martha's mother and the executrix of Mrs Lloyd's will. Martha visited and travelled with her elderly friend, spending several weeks caring for Mrs Dundas in the time leading up to her death in 1812.

Mrs. Fowle—There are recipe contributions from at least three Mrs Fowles in Martha's book. The earlier entries are most likely from Martha's aunt, Jane Fowle (née Craven), who married Revd Thomas Fowle of Kintbury in 1763. She died in 1798. Later entries are probably from Martha's sister Eliza Fowle (née Lloyd), who married her cousin Revd Fulwar Craven Fowle in 1788. She died in 1839. Sequenced in between these contributions is one from Mrs C. Fowle. She was probably Honoria Fowle (née Townsend), who married Martha's cousin Charles Fowle in 1799. She died in 1823.

Mrs. Lefroy—Anne Lefroy (née Brydges) was the wife of Revd I.P. George Lefroy and lived at Ashe near Steventon. A great friend and mentor of the young Jane Austen, Madam Lefroy died in a riding accident in December of 1804. This contributor could not be Jane's niece Anna Lefroy (née Austen) because her marriage to Ben Lefroy did not take place until November 1814. The sequence of entries contradicts this idea. It is possible that this is Mrs J.H. George Lefroy (née Sophia Cottrell), who married Ben Lefroy's elder brother. Her husband succeeded his father as rector of Ashe in 1806. Sophia Lefroy would have been the closest neighbour of Martha's sister Mary at Steventon—and Martha visited Steventon several times in 1806 before her move to Southampton.

Lady Williams—Jane Williams (née Cooper) was Jane Austen's cousin and schoolmate, who died tragically in a road accident on 9 August 1798. Martha may have visited with Lady Williams when she stayed at Steventon beginning in September of 1796 while her husband Sir Thomas was at sea.

Miss Lawrence—She may have been related to Mrs Lawrence, who, with the Miss Debarys, called on Mary (née Lloyd) Austen when she visited Cheltenham in September 1816. Nothing more definitive on this contributor has been found.

Mrs Wroughton—Mrs Wroughton's name appears in a list of opinions on Jane Austen's *Emma*;[16] there were generations of Wroughtons from Martha's girlhood home county of Berkshire. Mrs Wroughton's two-line recipe for 'Garlic Vinegar' could have come from a family friend of the Lloyds or the Fowles.

Miss Susan Debary—Martha's family may have befriended the Debarys during the Lloyds' years at Ibthorpe, located just west of the Debary home in Hurstbourne Tarrant. Martha and Susan stayed for a time at Deane to help Mary (née Lloyd) Austen during the birth of James-Edward in November of 1798. Jane described Susan Debary in a letter: 'She looks much as she used to do, is netting herself a gown in worsteds, and wears what Mrs. Birch would call a <u>pot hat</u>. A short and compendious history of Miss Debary!'[17] Martha visited the Debarys in Hurstbourne on several occasions. At one point, Jane wondered if Martha might marry Susan's brother, Revd Peter Debary. In the late 1970s author Peggy Hickman considered if the vicar of Mrs Austen's rhymed pudding recipe referred to Revd Debary,[18] but that entry appears too early in Martha's book to support this suggestion.

Cap^tn: Austen—Captain Francis William Austen was the elder seafaring brother of Jane Austen. He and his wife shared their Southampton home with Frank's mother, sisters and Martha Lloyd from 1807 to 1809. Five years after the death of Frank's first wife, Martha and Frank married in 1828 and shared a home for nearly fifteen years until Martha's death in 1843.

M^rs. Craven—Considering where these recipes appear in the sequence, they are not likely to have been handed down from Martha's grand-mother, Elizabeth Craven (née Stapes). This contributor is most likely Mrs Catherine Craven (née Hughes), the second wife of Martha's uncle, Revd John Craven. The couple married in 1799 and lived at Barton Court, Kintbury. John died in 1804. Years later, his widow lived at Speen Hill. Martha visited Mrs Craven at both homes. Mrs Craven also visited Chawton Cottage in July of 1813 and took an evening walk from the Great House with Martha, Jane and her niece Fanny Knight.

Mr Hartley—There are four sequential contributions from Mr Hartley, all culinary. Although we know nothing specific about Mr Hartley, the sequence of entries indicates that his contributions were made before 1812, the year Mrs Dundas died. Martha's sister Mary copied the Hartley recipe for Veal Soup into her pocketbook in 1836. The only wording difference is that she attributed the recipe 'From Mr L. Hartley', so clearly he was known to the Lloyd sisters.[19]

Miss Sharpe—Anne Sharp(e) was governess of Edward Austen's children at Godmersham from 1804 to 1806. Miss Sharpe accompanied Edward and his family on their September 1805 holiday to Worthing where they met up with Martha, Mrs Austen, Jane and Cassandra. Miss Sharpe visited Chawton Cottage in 1815 and 1820 during the years Martha lived there.

M^rs^. Sawbridge—She may have been the wife of Revd Henry Sawbridge, rector of Welford Parish near Newbury, Berkshire, the county where Martha grew up and with which she maintained connections throughout her life.

M^rs^. H^ry^. Austen—Jane Austen's brother Henry married twice and Martha was familiar with both women. His first wife Eliza de Feuillide Austen (née Hancock) died in April of 1813. Henry married Eleanor (née Jackson) in 1820. Because this entry falls late in the sequence and close to the final contributions from Mrs George Austen, it is most likely that these recipes came from Eleanor.

M^rs^. Hulbert—Family friends of the Lloyds, the Hulberts hosted both Martha and her sister Mary at their home at Speen Hill near Newbury, Berkshire. Likewise, the Hulberts visited the Lloyd sisters at both Chawton and Steventon. Mrs Hulbert died on 21 January 1840.

Dr. Turton—It is doubtful that Martha knew Dr Turton personally, so this is more likely a reference rather than a direct contribution. In addition to publishing *A Medial Glossary* (1797), Dr William Turton (1762–1835) published *A Treatise on Cold and Hot Baths* (1803), and *Some Observations on Consumption* (1813), which also encompassed various chronic diseases. The Montagu family seems to have known Dr Turton. Their household book contains a 'Mixture of burnt Spunge that Ly. M. Montagu took' by Dr. Turton's prescription 'after a Cough & Inflamation in the Lungs'.[20]

*M*ʳˢ. *Raymond*—This contributor was probably a distant relation of Mr Jemmet Raymond of Barton Court, Kintbury. Martha's maternal grandmother, Elizabeth Craven (née Staples), married Mr Raymond soon after the death of her first husband. She died in 1773 and had no issue from her second marriage. Martha was often at Kintbury to visit her sister, Eliza Fowle, and more specifically at Barton Court to visit family friend Mrs Dundas. Martha may have become acquainted with a Mrs Raymond in the area.

Ly. Bridges—Fanny, Lady Bridges (née Fowler) was the wife of Sir Brook Bridges, 3rd Bt of Goodnestone Park. Her daughter Elizabeth married Jane Austen's brother Edward. Lady Bridges died in 1825.

*M*ʳˢ. *E: Knight*—Given the sequence of the entries, this contributor was the wife of Edward Knight II, Mary Dorothea (née Knatchbull). The couple eloped on 13 May 1826 and took up permanent residence at Chawton House that summer. She died in 1838. The contributor cannot be the wife of Edward Austen Knight, as Hickman suggests,[21] because Edward did not take the surname Knight until 1812, four years after the death of his wife.

*M*ʳ. *Jenkins. 1829*—This contributor enjoys the distinction of having the only dated entry in Martha's book. Even without the date, the placement of his 'Saline draft' tells us that it was recorded after the bulk of the other entries. The identity of Mr Jenkins remains something of a mystery. We know that a Mrs Jenkins and Mrs Harwood called on Fanny Knight when she was at Steventon in November of 1809. In 1813, a Miss Jenkins was included in a Steventon dinner invitation from Martha's sister Mary. Given that Mr Jenkins's contribution was medicinal, he may have been a local apothecary.

*M*ʳˢ. *S: Terry*—Maria-Bridget Terry (née Seymer) was the wife of Stephen Terry and lived in Wyards near Chawton from 1811 to 1815.

Mrs Austen and granddaughter Fanny Knight called on her in May and June of 1813 during the time Martha was living at Chawton Cottage. This entry appears late in the sequence, so clearly Martha maintained the connection for some time afterwards.

C. Dexter Esqr—This was the husband of Martha's niece Mary Jane Dexter (née Fowle), Lt Christopher Dexter. He died whilst voyaging home from India accompanied by his wife. Years later, Martha remembered his widow with a legacy via Francis Austen's will.

Making connections
to Jane Austen

Jane Austen readers could certainly be tempted to make instant connections between the famous author and *Martha Lloyd's Household Book*.
Is this the actual White Soup mentioned in *Pride and Prejudice*? Have
we found the 'Receipt' for 'some excellent orange Wine'[1] that Jane
requested just months before her death? Of course, Jane never told
us whether any of these recipes inspired her words, but since she and
Martha shared several homes and similar experiences, it is natural to
explore the possibilities.

There is nothing specific in Martha's book to indicate Jane's favourite
foods. It would be astounding if a marginal note read 'Jane gobbled this
up!', similar to how she described herself 'devouring some cold Souse'.[2]
There are no hints from the most worn or stained pages of Martha's
manuscript, but we can amuse ourselves by drawing many connections
between the author's works and these recipes. By simply paging through
Martha's household book, we can catch glimpses of Jane Austen living
between the lines.

Pride and Prejudice is considered to be Jane Austen's most famous
novel, and its most memorable food reference comes from Mr Bingley.
He promises to host a ball at Netherfield, 'and as soon as Nicholls has
made white soup enough I shall send round my cards'.[3] Although Jane
could have sipped any version of the velvety, cream-based soup at the
balls mentioned in her letters, Martha's recipe is a likely candidate for

the author's favourite. But there was another White Soup recipe within the Austen family. *The Knight Family Cookbook*, compiled by Mr Austen's kinfolk, includes a variation of White Soup with vermicelli added.[4] Readers will have to decide if they want to picture the spirited Lydia Bennet slurping up a few noodles in the presence of Bingley's aloof friend Mr Darcy.

Fashionable French flair

We can imagine Mr Darcy and his aunt, Lady Catherine de Bourgh, dining in the highest style at their respective homes of Pemberley and Rosings. Dinner, the afternoon main meal of the day, was served *à la française* in imitation of the French Court. Guests entered the dining room to see a table pre-set with the first course arranged symmetrically.

Jane Austen mentioned the popular White Soup in *Pride and Prejudice* and may have enjoyed the dish prepared from Martha Lloyd's recipe or from this version found in *The Knight Family Cookbook*, c.1793.

White Soup   197.

Take two Quarts of Strong Veal Broth, set it over a slow fire, put in two Handfuls of Vermacilli, & boile it tender, then put in half a pint of Creame with the yolks of 4 Eggs beat together, & let it but just boile or it will Curdle, & it shou'd be sent to Table imediately. —
N.B. you may add a 1/4 of a pound of Almonds pounded.

Iceing For a Cake.

Take if whites of - Eggs, beat them all the while if Cake is Bakeing; then sift in the finest Loaf Sugar, till it seems thick enough to lay on your Cake. For a pch Cake the whites of 3 Eggs, & a pound of Sugar will do: which if not thick enough, sift in more Sugar. When if Cake is

To transition to the second course, certain dishes were removed and replaced with others. These 'removes' were planned in a way to preserve the perfect symmetry of the table. Jane Austen captured this dining style in *Emma*, when the Woodhouses hosted a dinner party for the Eltons. The guests moved to the dining room when 'Dinner was on table'.[5] Earlier in the novel, when Emma dined at the Coles, 'the awkwardness of a rather long interval between the courses' interrupted her engaging conversation with Frank Churchill. Only when 'the table was again safely covered, when every corner dish was placed exactly right',[6] could Emma and Frank renew their tête-à-tête. Both Jane and Martha likely dined *à la française* at Chawton House during the years they lived at Chawton Cottage.

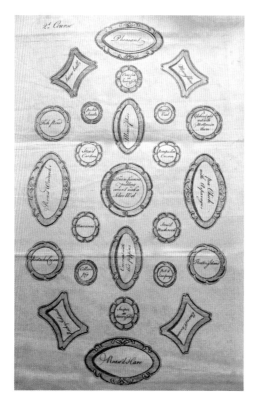

A table diagram from Elizabeth Raffald's *The Experienced English Housekeeper*, 1786, shows the symmetrical placement of dishes for dining *à la française*, the most fashionable style in Georgian England.

The dining table at Chawton House in 2005, set with the Knight family's 1813 Wedgwood china. Both Jane Austen and Martha Lloyd enjoyed meals in this room.

French fare signalled sophistication in Georgian Britain. We can find this attitude reflected in both Jane's writing and Martha's recipe collection. In *Pride and Prejudice*, heroine Elizabeth Bennet is made to feel beneath her company for many reasons, including her unrefined palate. The snobbish Mr Hurst, upon discovering Elizabeth to 'prefer a plain dish to a ragout, had nothing to say to her'.[7] Certainly Mr Darcy was familiar with French cuisine, or so Mrs Bennet thought: 'I suppose he has two or three French cooks at least.'[8] Martha collected recipes for a number of dishes with French names, ones Mr Hurst and Mr Darcy might enjoy: 'Blanch Mange', 'Jaune Mange', *crêpes* or 'Thin Cream Pancake, call'd Quire of paper', 'Fricassee Turnips' and 'A Harrico of Mutton'. Although Jane's letters show her appreciation for traditional English foods, they also reveal her recurring fascination for foods made with a French flair: 'I have had some ragout veal, and I mean to have some haricot mutton to-morrow.'[9]

Dinners for the middling sort

Despite their affinity for French fare, Jane and Martha's daily meals at Chawton Cottage probably resembled those from the respective Steventon and Enborne parsonages where they were raised. Their mothers probably arranged their modest meals according to the standard set previously in *The English Huswife*. The prudent woman was 'not to overreach herself with dishes beyond her status and budget, but to limit profusion to her purse … erring on the side of sustenance rather than show'.[10] Unlike the expansive courses laid out for the wealthy, tables for the middling sort were set economically with three to five dishes. This simplified style was recorded in one of Jane's letters from Steventon: 'Mr. Lyford was here yesterday; he came while we were at dinner, and partook of our elegant entertainment. I was not ashamed at asking him to sit down to table, for we had some pease-soup, a sparerib, and a pudding.'[11] Martha collected two recipes for 'Pease Soup' along with ten recipes for sweet or savoury puddings. Jane might have envisioned similar meals for Mr and Mrs Collins at Hunsford Parsonage in *Pride and Prejudice*, and for the disadvantaged Dashwoods at Barton Cottage in *Sense and Sensibility*.

Other examples of simple and abundant country foods permeate Jane's writing and Martha's household book. It is easy to envision Mrs Austen's Steventon dairy producing pails of milk, pints of cream and pounds of butter, inspiring young Jane's food-laden *Lesley Castle*. Here Charlotte Lutterell describes a surprising scene: 'my Sister came running to me in the Store-room with her face as White as a Whipt syllabub.'[12] Martha's trifle recipe features a mound of syllabub whipped 'as light as possible to cover the whole the higher it is piled the handsomer it looks'.[13] In *Mansfield Park*, Aunt Norris criticizes the Grants for 'the quantity of butter and eggs that were regularly consumed in the house'.[14] She might be shocked by Martha's recipe for 'A good Cheese cake with Curd' requiring nearly three-quarters of a pound of butter and eight eggs.[15]

When we see Martha's instructions 'To make Hams', we can appreciate the effort Mrs Austen made for one of her seafaring sons. 'My Mother has undertaken to cure six Hams for Frank;—at first it was a distress, but now it is a pleasure.'[16] Martha's recipe called for two 15-pound legs of pork to be coated repeatedly with a dry rub of salt and brown sugar. With a similar recipe, Mrs Austen would have to make sure the Castle Square cook turned and recoated the hams daily for a period of three weeks.[17]

Wise in culinary ways

Clearly Martha and Mrs Austen were knowledgeable in ways to instruct a cook, but Jane also demonstrated her share of kitchen wisdom— perhaps learned in girlhood at her mother's side. Despite Jane's eventual eagerness to ease her mind from 'the torments of rice puddings and apple dumplings',[18] her writing is seasoned with culinary references. Jane wrote to Cassandra about some disappointing black butter that 'proved not at all what it ought to be;—it was neither solid, nor entirely sweet. … It was made you know when we were absent.'[19] Obviously Jane thought that she and her sister could have made better. But Jane could rely on Martha to oversee the making of 'A Rice Pudding' using the recipe in her household book.

In another letter to Cassandra, Jane used her walk to the Alton butcher to specify her brother's arrival time: 'by the time that I had made the sumptuous provision of a neck of Mutton on the occasion, they drove into the Court—but lest you should not immediately recollect in how many hours a neck of Mutton may be certainly procured, I add that they came a little after twelve.'[20] Jane helped with the marketing and knew how to select appropriate cuts of meat. A number of Martha's recipes call for mutton, specifically the neck, breast meat, broth or suet.

Jane Austen's novels are likewise sprinkled with culinary references. In *Northanger Abbey*, General Tilney eats heartily at his son's table, being 'little disconcerted by the melted butter's being oiled'.[21] Martha would have recognized the reference to the butter sauce and understood Hannah Glasse's advice 'to keep shaking your pan one way, for fear it should oil'.[22] Martha's recipe 'To make Cabbage Pudding' finishes with 'melted butter' sauce.[23]

Nowhere is Jane's culinary knowledge more apparent than in the detailed pork conversation in *Emma*.[24] The heroine and Mr Woodhouse discuss Emma's gift of pork to the Bates household. In the span of three paragraphs, Jane includes fourteen examples of food seasonality, cooking terms and butcher's cuts of meat. Most of these examples can be found in Martha's recipe collection. Although Jane's letters do not mention any butchering performed at Chawton Cottage, visitors can still see the livestock hoisting winch hanging from the bakehouse rafters. About the time Jane was completing *Emma* at the cottage, she wrote to niece Caroline: 'Grandmama & Miss Lloyd will be by themselves, I do not exactly know what they will have for dinner, very likely some pork.'[25] Martha collected six recipes for curing, pickling or preparing pork.

Peeking inside Chawton Cottage

Using Jane's letters and Martha's book, we can piece together typical days at the cottage. A beautiful spring afternoon could find Jane strolling through the orchard: 'You cannot imagine—it is not in Human Nature to imagine what a nice walk we have round the Orchard … I hear today that an Apricot has been detected on one of the Trees.'[26] Only two days earlier, she wrote of expecting 'a great crop of Orleans plumbs—but not many greengages—on the standard scarcely any—three or four dozen perhaps against the wall'.[27] All the ripened fruits from the cottage grounds would work well for Martha's recipe 'To preserve fruit of any kind'. Jane also described a good yield of gooseberries that would come in handy for Martha's jam-like 'Gooseberry Cheese' or 'Green Gooseberry Wine'. But Jane noticed having 'fewer Currants than I thought at first.—We must buy currants for our Wine.—'[28] Martha's instructions 'To Make Currant Wine' do

Visitors to Jane Austen's House today can picture Jane and Martha Lloyd walking through the grounds that once featured fruit trees and a kitchen garden filled with vegetables and herbs.

not indicate the quantity of currants, but to yield each gallon of juice she would have to begin with many pounds of fruit.

Through Jane's correspondence, we can watch the seasons unfold, from spring peas to summer vegetables, and eventually to autumn when bushels of apples could be transformed into a number of Martha's dishes, including 'A Baked Apple Pudding' and sweet 'Apple Snow' with fruit and meringue whipped 'for a full hour until it all looks like snow'.[29]

Jane did not hesitate to voice her opinion of their cook: 'Her Cookery is at least tolerable;—her pastry is the only deficiency.'[30] This was concerning because Jane felt that 'Good apple pies are a considerable part of our domestic happiness.'[31] Perhaps Martha helped the cook by sharing Mrs Austen's recipe for 'Brised Crust' or *Pâte Brisée* (what we might call shortcrust or piecrust).

Jane Austen's favourites

All the blooming fruit trees, shrubs and garden flowers around the cottage attracted bees from Cassandra's hive. Whenever Jane was away, she was glad to get Cassandra's reports of bee productivity: 'I am happy to hear of the Honey.—I was thinking of it the other day.'[32] Honey is the principal ingredient in mead, Jane's favourite drink. Martha's recipe 'To Make Mead' calls for 4 pounds of honey for every gallon of water. Letters between the Austen sisters frequently mention the honey output and various stages of mead making: 'Cook does not think the Mead in a State to be stopped down.'[33] Ironically, Martha's book does not include a recipe for her own favourite drink, spruce beer—but Jane mentioned it in *Emma*. The character Harriet Smith kept among her *'Most precious treasures'* a tiny pencil that Mr Elton brought out 'to make a memorandum in his pocket-book; it was about spruce beer'.[34] Perhaps Jane had included the reference as a small homage to her dear friend.

Martha also saved a recipe for Jane's beloved 'Toasted Cheese'. The simple dish must have been known within the family as Jane's favourite, because brother-in-law and likely suitor Edward Bridges arranged for it: 'It is impossible to do justice to the hospitality of his attentions towards me; he made a point of ordering toasted cheese for supper entirely on my account.'[35] We can imagine Martha thoughtfully planning the dish eight years later at Chawton Cottage, as Jane wrote *Mansfield Park*. Jane's exhausted heroine Fanny Price took the first invitation to go to bed: 'leaving all below in confusion and noise again, the boys begging for toasted cheese'.[36]

Planning the garden

Mrs Austen liked to plant and dig up her own potatoes, so surely they became a part of the cottage garden plan. Asparagus, beets, cabbages, carrots, cauliflower, cucumbers, garlic, lettuce, onions and spinach were all staples in the kitchen garden—and all appear in Martha's book. Along with fresh fruits, this 'garden stuff' balanced the eighteenth-century diet rich in meats, butter and cream. Abundant vegetable crops could stretch through the winter months if dehydrated, as with 'To dry Mushrooms', or pickled, as with 'To Pickle Pattigonian' cucumbers. Of course Martha also collected recipes for fresh vegetables headed straight to the dinner table. Both vegetable and meat dishes were enhanced with herbs from the kitchen garden, especially marjoram, mint, parsley, rosemary, savory and thyme.

Useful preparations and remedies

Garden plans were also made with household preparations and remedies in mind, and Martha filled roughly a quarter of her book with recipes for these. When Henry Austen visited the cottage, Jane warned Cassandra: 'His Stomach is rather deranged. You must keep him in Rhubarb & give him plenty of Port & Water.'[37] Stalks of rhubarb were used for cooking, but the roots were used medicinally. Cutting flowers and herbs made sweet 'Pot-pouri' for rooms, while lavender buds and rose petals were distilled to make refreshing waters and softening lotions, such as Captain Austen's 'Milk of Roses'. Beeswax from Cassandra's hive was essential for 'A good salve for sore Lips', contributed to Martha's book by Mrs Fowle.

Some of Martha's recipes called for key ingredients procured from the Alton apothecary and later combined with items from the cottage. To make writing ink, Martha needed to buy gallic acid, iron sulphate and gum Arabic. These were beaten together in a mortar then mixed with beer and sugar. We can only wonder if Martha followed this formula[38] to fill Jane's inkwell. At one point, Jane wrote from Chawton describing 'an Off & on Cold … I increase it by walking out & cure it by staying within.'[39] Jane may have benefited from 'D^r: Turton's receipt for a Cold' using salt of ammoniac, Tolu balsam, almond oil and common saltpetre mixed with water from the courtyard pump.

One last recipe

No matter how many remedies Martha collected, nothing in contemporary medicine could cure Jane's final illness, now suspected to have been Addison's disease.[40] About six months before her death, Jane's health seemed to rally—enough for her to write to friend Alethea Bigg: 'We remember some excellent orange Wine at Manydown, made from Seville oranges, entirely or chiefly—& should be very much obliged to you for the receipt.'[41] Although Martha's book includes two recipes for orange wine, neither can be the one Jane requested. Martha's first orange wine recipe appears near the beginning of her book on page 17. This entry was most likely recorded during the mid-1790s. The second orange wine recipe appears somewhat later on page 79, but was contributed by Mrs C. Fowle. Both recipes include the tart Seville oranges that Jane remembered, but the specific 'Receipt' from Alethea Bigg has probably been lost to the ages. Of the 196 recipes recorded in Martha's book, roughly 45 were contributed by Austen and Lloyd family members, or by their friends and acquaintances. Whether or not these exact recipes were prepared for Jane Austen, they provide us with a fascinating perspective of the time and manner in which she lived.

Martha Lloyd's Household Book

Cookery

interest

1

A A Pease Soup

Take two quarts of pease boil them down to a pulp
strain them, put half a p'd of Butter into a stew
pan, Sallery, half an Onion, & stew them till
tender. Then put two anchovies, pounded
peper, Salt, mint and Paßley each a small handful & Spinach & beat of each a small Quantity
half a spoonful of Sugar. the Soup to be boiled
as thick as you like it and the Whole to be all
to-gether boiled up & Dished.

To Make light Wigs

Take a p'd & half of flour & half a pint of
Made warm, mix these together, and
let it stand by the fire half an hour, then
half a p'd of Butter & half a
these in the paste and make it into Wigs with
little flour as poßible. let the oven
& They will rise very

A pound Cake

Take a pound of fine flour well dried, then
take a pound of Butter, & work it very well with
your hands, till it is Soft, then work into it half
p[d] of y[e] Sugar, then beat 10 eggs puting a way
half the Whites, then work them also into your
Butter and Sugar, then strew your flour into your Butter
Sugar, & eggs, by little & little, till all be in,
then Strew in 2 oz: of Carraway Seeds, butter your
Pan, and bake it in a quick Oven, — an hour &
half will bake it. ——————————

Wallnut Catchup

Take green Wallnuts and pound them to a
paste then put to every hundred two quarts of
vinegar with a handful of Salt put it altogether
in an~~handful~~ earthen pan keeping it stirring for
eight days. then Squeese it through a coarse Cloth,
& put it into a well tined Saucepan, when it
begins to boil skim it as long as any scum rises
and add to it some Cloves, mace, sliced Ginger,
sliced nutmeg, jamaica pepper corns, sliced
horse radish, with, ~~a~~ a few shalots, let this
have one boil up, then pour it into an
earthen pan, and after it is cold bottle it
up, dividing the ingredients equally into
each bottle. ———

A Pease Soup

Take five or six Cucumbers pared and sl[ice]
the white part of as many Cofs Lettice a sprig
or two of Mint; two or three Onions, some pep[per]
a little salt a full pint of young Pease a li[ttle]
Parsley half a pound of butter put them alto[gether]
in a sauce pan to stew in their own liquor for a[n]
hour and half or fill they are quite tender; the[n]
boil as many old Pease pulp them through a
cullender and mix them in a quart of the li[quor]
or more as you like it for thickness when the her[bs]
are stewed enough put them in and serve it u[p]

A receipt for a Pudding

If the Vicar you treat,
You must give him to eat,
A pudding to hit his affection;
And to make his repast,
By the canon of taste,
Be the present receipt your direction.

first take two pounds of Bread,
Be the crumb only weigh'd,
For crust the good house-wife refuses;
The proportion you'll guess,
May be made more or less,
To the size that each family chuses.

Then its sweetness to make
Some currants you take
And Sugar of each half a pound

Be not Butter forgot
And the quantity sought
Must the same with your currants be four

Cloves & Mace you will want,
With rose water I grant,
And more savory things if well chosen;
Then to bind each ingredient,
Youll find it expedient,
Of Eggs to put in half a dozen.

Some milk dont refuse it,
But boiled ere you use it,
A proper hint this for its maker;
And the whole when compleat,
In a pan clean and neat,
With care recommend to the baker.

In praise of this pudding,
I vouch it a good one,
Or should you suspect a fond word;
To every Guest,
Perhaps it is best,
Two puddings should smoke on the board.

Two puddings.—yet—no,
For if one will do,
The other comes in out of season;
And these lines but obey,
nor can any-one say,
That this pudding's with-out rhyme or reason.

To make Hams *as Portsdown Lodge half the quantity of Sugar and rather more Salt than the Receipt states*

Take Two legs of Pork, each leg weighing about
pounds, rub them well over with two oz: of Salt,
finely beaten, let them lie a day and night the
take two pound of Brown Sugar, one pound &
half of common Salt, mix them together and
your Hams with it, let them lie three Weeks t
and rub them in the pickle every day. —

Calves feet Jelly

Take a set of Calves feet boil them to a Str
Jelly the whites of 16 eggs five oranges & ha
Lemons a stick of Cinnamon two bay leaves
a sprig of Rosemary sweeten it to your taste
if you cannot get oranges put five Lemons
pare the peels in some of the Jelly boiling
hot an hour before you make them.

A Carraway Cake

Take 3 p.^d of flour, 2 p.^d of Butter ~~rubbed~~
bed into the flour an ounce & half of Carraway
ds 12 spoonfuls of Milk, 12 spoonfuls of Yeast, 12
lks of eggs 4 whites, beat all these well together
t them into your flour stiring it very well, let
stand by the fire side a quarter of an hour to
se. when the oven is hot strew in the carraway's
tiring it all the time. then butter your pan and
ut in your cake. an hour and half will bake it.
N B Put in a pound of Sugar

To bake a buttock of Beef

To a Buttock of Beef of 18 pounds take 2 q.^d of common
salt, half a p.^d of coarse sugar, & two oz. of Salt petr
let them be well rubbed in, and turn the beef every day
for a fortnight. then roll it up very tight with
eggars tape; put it into a deep pan and cover
t with equal parts of red wine and water. bake
five hours take it out of the Liquor when it is
cold. it will keep six or 8 weeks.

A very good way to dry Beef

Take eight ribs of Beef, lay it on a stone
board, & rub a little Salt upon it let it li
three days, then rub well into it 2 oz: of Sa
petre made hot at the fire, let it lie ten da
turning it once in two days, and put a little
Salt to it as you see it wanting then hang i
~~dry in to~~ dry in the Kitchen, but not too nea
the fire. when dry keep it in Malt.

Fish Sause.

Crawfish shells pounded in a stone morta
put some thin gravy to them, a bit of Cinn
& a bit of crust of Bread, stew this altogether til
tis strong, then strain it off and mix it wit
Butter and anchovey, lobster shells will do,
well as Crawfish.

Blanch Mange

Take half an oz: of Bitter Almonds, blanch
'em & pound them very fine, then put them into
half a pint of good Cream with Sugar then
ke half an oz: of Isinglass, & put boiling upon
half a pint of new milk let it stand to be
old then put it altogether, boil it about 3
minutes, keep it stirring all the while, then strai
t into something, keep it stirring till cold, the
ut it into cups, which must be wetted that the
ay turn out easily.————

New College Puddings

To make a dozen of new College puddings take
o pounds of grated bread, half a pound of Bee
et minced very fine, half a pound of Curr'ant
egg's a quarter of a pound of Sugar a little
utmeg one spoonful of rose or orange flowr
ter, mix them all well together then

clarify half a pound of Butter, put them
into it & set them over a gentle fire keep
them ~~stirring~~ turning as you find them
brown they will be done in about 20 minu
serve them up in butter; or wine & Butter

To Make Mead

To every Gallon of Water, put four pound of
honey, & for 20 Gallons add as follows, two oz:
Nutmeg, half an oz: of Mace half an oz: of Clove
2 oz of Race-Ginger, all just bruised, and sew
up in a ~~linen bag~~ Linen bag; then add a la
handful, of Sweet-briar with the above. boil
all together one hour skiming it all the time
boils; then strain it off as you do Wort, add a
Barm to it, if it does not Work tun it and b
stand a day or two, then add the juice of 6 g
Lemons, with the rind of them. and your

of spices in the barrel stop it up close for
o or 12 Months then bottle it for use. you
may add more spices if you like it. ———

To make Turtle

Take a Calves head, dress it as you do the feet.
t it lay in cold water for some time, then boil
in a Cloth very tender, then cut it into
mall pieces, make your gravy of veal and beef
inced very small, put it into a jar with a little
eet herbs, water, peper, & mace, Chian, Butter &
ion, add your Gravy to your meat, & put in
lf a pint of Madeira Wine, 2 anchovies worked
in flour & butter, to make it as thick as you
ke it, the yolks of 12 Eggs boild hard, the brains
ade green with spinage, and beet root fryed.
The force meat balls for the turtle. take the
eet bread of the veal or some lamb cut into sma
ieces, with twice as much suet, & some crumbs
bread, two eggs, salt, mace, lemon peel.

16   a little pepper, & an ~~an~~ onion boiled, beat
all together for some time, then take the yol
of 3 hard eggs, cut small, and put it to it,
make it into large Balls and fry them. ——

To make Lemon Cheese cakes

Take ~~haff~~ half a pᵈ of almonds blanch'd in cold wa
let stand all night, beat fine with Orange flower w
take half a pᵗ of fine sugar, then take the Peal
of two Lemons paired very thin, boil it in water til
they are very tender & not bitter; then beat it very f
in a Mortar with the sugar, then mix it with
almonds, take eight eggs leaving out half the whites;
3 qᵗ of a pᵗ of butter melted & let it be cold, then mix
it altogether bake it in fine paste in small patty p
put some sugar in your paste. ——

To Pot Beef

Take the lean of fat beef & lay it in Salt Petre 48 h
thin bake it in an earthen pot with butter or f
shred beef Suet, when it is baked, take ~~take~~ the gra
from it & ~~take~~ break it in pieces with your hands & se
with pepper salt Cloves & Mace & Nutmeg then, i

into the pot again & fill it up again as before   17

set it into the oven and bake it again then put

it clarified butter; this will keep a Year. _____

To make Gingerbread

Take four Pints of flour rub into it 3 quarters of

lb of butter 2 oz: of Ginger a Nutmeg, one oz: of

[ca]raway seeds a quarter of a pint of Brandy 2 lb of

[tre]acle, mix it altogether; & let it lay till it grows

[sti]ff then roll it out, & cut it into cakes, you may

[ad]d what sweet-meats you please. _____

To make Cabbage Pudding

[Ta]ke the lean of Venison or Veal chopt very small, put

[to] it beef suet chopt small then take a piece of

[ca]bbage half boiled chopt it & mix it with the meat;

[sea]son it with pepper salt & nutmeg two yolks of eggs

[the]n take the Cabbage leaves & dip them into the

[bo]iling water & put your meat into them, the

[big]ness you would have them with thread they must

[boil t]wo hours then serve them up with melted butter

To make Orange Wine

[Take] 2 Gallons of Water let it boil an hour, when it is

[co]ld have ready a hundred & twelve lb of Malaga raisons

[pic]ked, & chopt small; when the water is quite cold

[pu]t it on the raisons let it stand a fortnight stirring it

[on]ce every day, then strain the liquor from the raisons

18 squeeze them very hard, let the liquor run throu
a hair sive then have ready a   Civil Oranges th
pare'd very thin squeeze the juice of the Oranges up
the Peels & put that and the liquor into the Vese
and when it has done working stop it up you may
stop it bottle it when fine which will be in a
two Months

Cowslip Wine

Take eight gallons of water boil it and let it stand
be cold a little cool then put into it 8 Gallons of cowsly
flowers picked and 8 lemons sliced, stir it together well an
so do for 5 or 6 days then strain it out and add to this qu
a quarter of a 100 of Lisbon Sugar stir it well together &
spread a toast of brown bread with new yeast on both su
& put to it let it work as long as it stood before, & then
it into a vesel of the same size when fine draw it but
to soon.

To Make Currant Wine

Pick the Currants off the stems, and pound them; & to
gallon of water liquor put two quarts of spring water,
two p⁴ of of Sugar Barrel it up watch it till it is clear
for all these Wines must be taken just in the nick of t
when they are first clear or else they are spoiled & bottle
out if you would have it to drink soon you must put t
let Sugar in it, in some weather it will not be clear in
vesel till it has stood to long for the body. so you must dr

it of into bottles & in a week after decant it into other / 9
bottles putting a lump of Sugar into every bottle. _____

To Pickel Saphire

Take samphire & put it into a brass pot & to each peck of Samphire
put in 2 quarts of water white wine Vinegar & on quart of
water lay something of weight to keep it under the water, &
paste the pot lid down close that no steam may come out
let it not boil to long for it will not be so well set it of the fire
till it is cold, then put it in an earthen jar & the same
liquor to it, put no salt. _____

To Pickle 3e Dutch Plum or White Dam

To a Gallon of White wine Vinegar put 3 pints
of Mustard 5 heads of garlick a good handful of
shellotts a good handful of horse-radish. when it is
sliced three races of Ginger sliced half an oz of
Jamaica pepper & what salt you think fit _____

The Plumbs must be gather'd before they are
quite fat riper when they are turning yellow
they must be cut a little on one side to let in
the liquor put them in raw, your mustard must
be made as to eat. _____ You may do Mellons or cucumbers
the same way only take out the inside and rub
them with Salt _____

To Pickle Onions

Take half a peck of the smallest Onions you
can get, peal them and put them into fair wa[ter]
& salt let them stand all Night then boil the[m]
a little in fresh water & skim them very wel[l]
make the pickle as for Cucumbers, let the Onio[ns]
& the pickle be cold when you put them toge[ther]
it is the best way to still the Vinegar with [the]
Spices in it. _____

To Make Hartshorn Jelly.

To four oz: of hartshorn shavings, one quart [of]
Water & boil it dry, then put another quart
of water & boil it till it will Jelly, ye whites [of]
two Eggs & beat them to a froth with the juice
of a lemon & half an ~~ys of~~ orange a stick of
Cinnamon & sugar to your taste, run your Jelly
through a bag & let it stand to be a little cool [as]
you put your eggs to it then boil it till it loo[ks]
clear or the eggs begin to sink then run it thr[ough]
the bag till it is quite Clear. _____

To Make Fish Sauce for keeping 21

Take a pint of Port Wine, 12 Anchovies, a
Quarter of a pint of Vinegar, as much beaten
pepper, as will lay on a half Crown; 2 or 3 Cloves,
as much Mace; a Nutmeg, a small Onion,
bay leaves, a little Thyme, & parsley, 2 bits
of horse radish; put it all together in a Sauce
pan, and let it simmer, till all the Anchovies are disolved; then strain it off, and when
cold, bottle it up; it will keep half a year
in a cool place. mix it with Melted butter
the quantity according to your taste.

To Make a rich thick Cheese

Take seven quarts of Cream, ten gallons of
Milk, let them be cool run; then break it gently
take out the whey, put it into a great thick
Vate with a hoop in it; lay the Curd gently into
the Vate, lay a small weight on it, press it gently
for an hour & half; then take it out, & slice it
thin, put it into a tub of Cold water; let it

22 lay a quarter of an Hour, then take it ou[t]
make it very dry with clean cloaths; then p[ut]
in a pint of cream (it must be very thi[ck]
after it is broke in small pieces as big a[s]
a Wallnut, mix them, then put it gently [in]
the Vate, lay a pound weight upon it, pre[ss]
gently by degrees till night with more we[ight]
then put it into the press: next morning
turn it, salt it & put it into the press
again; at night turn it & salt it a little
more, put it into the press: next mornin[g]
bind it about with fillets, set it to dry ge[ntly]
change the fillets daily. ———

To Make Wafers

Take eight eggs, leaving out half the wh[ite]
& mix them with a pint of skim Milk; m[ake]
it into a thick batter, the same as f[or] pan[cakes]
put in four or five spoonfuls of new Yeast,
grated nutmeg, near half a p.d of Butter m[elt]
ted, beat it well to-gether; you may warm [the]
Milk a little, it will rise the better;

To make a fine Cake

Take 2 pound of fine flour dried & sifted, a
[p]ound of butter rubing it into the flour, take
[a] pound of currants wash'd ~~water~~ & pick'd,
[a]nd set in an oven to dry, then mix them
[to] the flour after the butter, then take
[ca]ndid orrange peel lemon, sittron & Apricot
[of] each a quarter ~~a part~~ of a pound, a Nutmeg, & some ~~spice~~
[m]ace, mix them together & four eggs but two
[w]hites, beat the eggs well with two spoonfuls
[of] sack, & a pint of yeast, & a pint of cream,
[m]ild & let stand to be cold, then strain them
[&] make it into an indifferent ~~stiff~~ paste,
[ke]ep out some of the cream till you see
[ho]w it is; let it stand an hour before the
[fi]re to rise, & when the oven is hot turn
[it] into a hoop & work it with your hands,
[le]t the hoop be butter'd. Dont rub the
[b]utter to hard in the flour. ———

A Rice Pudding

Six ounces of rice flour, one quart of crea
mix it well together & boil it, put to it
half a pound of butter, half a pound of
sugar, & one nutmeg grated & then take
off; when cold beat six eggs whites & all
& put to it butter your dish before you
put it in. Bake it quick you may paste
your dish if you please. ____

To make scotch Collops

Take part of a leg of veal & cut it thin
into what shapes you please hack it with
the back of a knife till it but just hang
together fry it in fresh butter, put all into
your pan cold

For the Balls

Take double the quantity of suet you do of
meat & beat it very small, season it with
nutmeg salt pepper & anchovy to your tast
eggs according to the quantity of meat put cre

of bread mix all well together & make them
up some round & some long cut off the
Udder of the veal & stuff it with the same
as the balls truss it round & roast it,
& lay it in the middle of the dish. —

For the sauce

Take some bones or some meat put it in
water with a bundle of sweet herbs as
Thyme Margrom & savory & Onion a little
Mace & lemon peel, a little white wine
and thicken it up with flour & butter —

To stew Piggeons brown

Take a piece of fat & lean bacon, & a
piece of butter, let this brown in the stew
pan, & when you have stuff'd your Piggeons
put them into the pan & brown them,
when they are brown all over put to it an
onion a bundle of sweet herbs put to them
warm water enough to cover them, with
an anchovy, put the jiblets in it will
help the gravy, when it is enough strain it
& put to it a piece of butter & a little flour. —

To make Gooseberry Vinegar

Bruise gooseberries full ripe in a Mortar,
then measure them ~~& to every~~ & to every qua
of gooseberries put three quarts of water
first boild, & let it stand to be cold then
water to the gooseberries & let it stand 24
hours, then strain it through canvas & then fla
& to every gallon of this liquor put one pou
of feeding brown sugar, stir it well togethe
and barrel it up. At three quarters of a ye
it will be fit for use but if it stands longer i
is better. This Vinegar is like-wise good for
Pickles.

never stop down
your Barrel

To Hash a Calves Head

Boil y.e Calves head 'till the meat is near
enough for eating, take it up & cut it in pieces
then take half a pint of whitewine, & three
quarters of a pint of gravy or strong broth, put
in this liquor two anchovies, half a nutmeg,
a little mace. & a small onion stuck with
cloves, boil them up in the liquor a quarter of
an hour, then strain it, & let it ~~stand~~ boil
up again, when it does so throw in the meat
with a little salt to y.e taste, & some lemon
peel sliced fine, let it stew a little, & if you
please add sweet breads, make force meat
balls of veal, mix the brains with the yolk
of eggs, & fry them to lay for garnish; when
the Head is ready to be sent in, shake in a
bit of Butter. ————————

To Jugg Beef Steakes with Potatoes

Take rump Steakes, beat them well pepp
& salt them, then take a soup-pot, put
the bottom a little fresh ~~lard~~ butter, a
row of Stakes, a row of Potatoes, & so on 'te
'tis full; then fill some gravy or broth, ju
enough to cover it, let it stew for three h
then strain it all off & skim all the fat
from it; thicken it up with butter & flou
then put it over the staakes again, give
it one boil up, & taste if salt enough.

To make almond Cheese-cake

Take half a p. of blanch'd almon
rounded small with a spoonful of ro
flower water & half a pound of doub
refined sugar 10 yolks of Eggs well be
add the peels of two oranges or Lemon
which must be ~~beaten~~ boil'd very
tender then beat in a Mortar veryf
then mix them altogether & put in th

quarters of a pound of melted butter
being almost cold & bake it in good
crust. ——————————————

Lemon Mince Pies

Take a good Lemon, squeese out the
Juice; boil the pulp with the rind tender, & pound
it very fine; put to it three quarters
of a pound of currants, half a p.d of
Sugar; half an oz: of Orange flour
water a good glass of Mountain or
Brandy put ~~to it~~ in your juice with
half a Nutmeg a little Mace Citron
or candied Orange peel as you please
you must put three quarters of a p.d of
Beef Suet chopt very fine & mixed with
the Currants. ~~Half a doz: Apples chopt fine &~~
~~added to it, is a great improvement~~ ————

A good Cheese cake with curd

To. a p.d & half of Cheese curd
put 10 oz: of butter; beat both in a
Mortar till all looks like butter.

Then add a quarter of a pound of
Almonds beat fine ~~fine~~ with Orange
flower water; 3 quartes of a pound of
Sugar, 8 Eggs, half 3.e whites; a little
Mace pounded, & a little cream; bea
all together a quarter of an hour;
bake them in puff paste & in a quic
Oven. _____

Sauvages

Take a pound of veal, a pound of Por
& a pound of Suet; take the skin & f
from the pork, & Veal, & skin the Suet
Then put it together & chop it very fi
then put a little Thyme chopt, & sa
pepper & salt, & chop it altogethe
then mix it up with yolks of Eggs th
it may be stiff. _____

A Trifle

Take three naple Biscuits cut them in
Slices dip them in sack lay them in
the bottom of your dish ... there make
a custard of a pint of cream & five
eggs & put over them then make a
hipt Syllabub as light as possible
to cover the whole the higher it is
piled the handsomer it looks. —————

To make Elder wine

To two Gallons of Water put one
Gallon of Berries full ripe & three
pounds of Sugar to one Gallon of
Liquor first boil the water & the
Berries three quarters of an hour,
strain the Berries out then boil
only half the Sugar in the liquor a

quarter of an hour & skim it th
putt it boiling on the other part o
the Sugar in the tub you intend
work it in. Stir it well together le
it stand eight & forty hours, then
spread a toast with yeast on both
sides well & work it till it has a
good head skim off the Barm be
you turn it dont stop it down clo
for a week or more if your Barke
is full.

A Two-penny Pudding

Take 2 Spoonfuls of flour weted with cold mi
than added near a pint of Boiling with a
little grated Lemon peel four Eggs well b
to be put to it when cold with a Spoo
ful of Powder Sugar Boil it in a dish
3 Quarters of an hour

Soup Curry

37
Take a good Knuckle of Veal, put it up
to boil with a Couple of Onions stuck with
half a dozen Cloves. let it boil very gently
till the Veal is tender. then take it
out & cut it from the bone, into large
dice. then take two large spoonfuls of
rice; parch it before the fire, beat it
in a Mortar & put it through a Lawn
sieve, take two ounces of Butter, the flour
of Rice & a large Onion. choped small
put altogether into your stew pan, &
put to them the broth & the Meat which
you have cut from the bone. let simmer
very gently till the meat is enough. then
put into it two tea spoonfuls of _____
& season it with Chyan & black pepper _
your taste. some rice boil'd dry must be
_____ up in a separate dish with it.
the rice is to be boil'd in a large quantity

of Water and it must be thrown in
when the water is boiling very fast
with it a handful of Salt. ————

A good Sauce for fish, or any made
Dis
Take a pint of Port wine, twelve
anchovies, a quarter of a pint of
Vinegar, as much beaten pepper a w
as will lay on a Crown piece, two
three Cloves a little Mace, one nut.
a small Onion, two Bay leaves, a litt
Thyme & Parsley & two Bits of Horse-
radish; put all this in a sauce-pan
till all the anchovies are dissolv'd; then
strain it off & when cold bottle it. ——I
will keep half a Year in a Cool place
melt your Butter thick & put in of
this Mixture according to your pala

A Baked Apple Pudding

Take a Dozen of Pippins, pulp them through
a Cullender, take six eggs, Sugar enough
to make Sweet, the rhind of two Lemons
grated, a quarter of a p.d of Butter
melted without flour or water, Squeeze
the juice of two Lemons, let the apples
be cold before the ingredients are put
together make a puff paste in the
bottom of the dish. Half an Hour bakes
it.

Jaune Mange

Steep two Oz: of Isinglass an Hour in a
pint of Boiling water & if not dissolved
by that time set it over the fire till it
then strain it through a clean sieve
and let it stand a few minutes to settle,

40. then pour it into a Sauce pan & p[ut]
near a pint of whitewine & the juice
of two Oranges or one Lemon & the p[eel]
of one & the Yolks of eight eggs sweete[ned]
to your taste with Loaf Sugar, let i[t]
~~stand~~ over the fire, and keep it st[ir]
ring till it just boils up & then stra[in]
it off into cups which must be wette[d]
that they may turn out easily. ———

To make Soy

Take one hundred of Walnuts, when they are
fit to pickle, & pound them small as can
be, add two ~~spoonfuls~~ Handfuls of Salt,
the next day put a quart of the best vinegar to them, let them lie open to the Air
till they are quite black, stirring them
two or three times a day, then put a Quart
of Strong Beer, & boil it ten minutes, then
strain it off & let it stand till the next day
then pour off the clear, & to that add a
bottle of Port wine, & a head of Garlic cut
small, the peel of a Lemon, & a bundle of
sweet herbs, half a h.d of Anchovies; boil
all these together a quarter of an hour, then
strain it off, then put into it Mace & Jamaica
pepper of each half an ounce (whilst 'tis hot)
when cold bottle it, 'tis not fit for Use under

2 or 3 Months — Its excellent for all
brown gravies, it makes fine fish Sauce
& will keep 20 Years. _____

To make little Patties to fry
Take the kidney of a Loin of Veal or da
fat & all, shred it very small, season it
with a little Salt, Cloves & Nutmeg, all
beaten small, some Sugar & ye yolks of
two or three Eggs hard, minced very fine
mix all these together with a little sa
or Cream, put them into puff paste &
them. _____

Thin Cream Pancake, call'd Quire of paper

Take to a pint of cream eight eggs leaving
out two whites, three spoonfuls of fine flour
3 spoonfuls of Sack & one spoonful of Orange
flower water a little sugar a grated nutmeg,
& a quarter of a p:d of butter melted in the
cream, mingle all well together, mixing the
flour with a little cream at first that it
may be smooth: butter your pan for the
first Pancake, and let them run as thin as possible
to be whole; when one side is coulored it is enough,
take them carefully out of the pan, & strew some
fine sifted sugar between each. lay them as even
on each other as you can, this quantity will mak
twenty

Fish Sauce

Crawfish shels pounded in a stone Mortar
put some thin gravy to them, a bit of crust
of bread stew this altogether till it is very
strong then strain it off & mix it with
butter & anchovy.————

A very good Orange Pudding

Pare the Yellow rind of two fair Oranges
very thin that no part of the white comes off
with it or grate them with a nutmeg gra[ter]
add to it half a p.d of butter & the Yolks of [...]
Eggs beat altogether in a stone mortar till
all of a colour, then pour it into your dish
in which you have laid a sheet of puff pa[ste]
three quarters of an hour bakes it. ————

A Bread Pudding

Take half a p.d of bread, half a p.d of Suet,
half a p.d of currants, & half a p.d of Sugar, [...]
eggs, boil it between three & four hours. ——

Sauce for a Carp

Put into a quarter of a pint of good gravy
one Anchovy shred small, a race of ginger
bruised, a bit of thyme, a bit of bread crumbled
small, let this boil a little while, then put
in near a p:d of butter, some of which must
be mix'd with flour to make the sauce
thick, & when it has just boil'd as butter
does, put in a spoonful of catchup, the
blood of the Carp & half a Lemon squeeze'd,
take out the thime & ginger. The Carp must
be bled in two or three spoonfuls of red wine,
in a pewter plate, kept stirring all the time
they bleed; they must not be boil'd in much
more water than will cover them. You in
must put in above half a pint of vinegar
or varjuice varjuice in the water — you boil
them in, a bunch of sweet herbs, an onion a race
of ginger some bruised Lemon peel & a piece of
Lemon ———

Almond Cream

Blanch & beat half a p.d of Almonds & boil
them in a quart of Cream, then take the Wt:
of four Eggs well beat sweeten it to your
taste with sugar & with a little Orange
flower water add it to the cream & keep
it on the fire till ready to boil: keep it
stirring all the time. ____

To make Ollivers Biscuits

Take 8 p.d of flour, half a pint of ma-
beer barm take some milk & warm it a
little put it to your barm & lay a spu-
let it lay for one hour then take a qua-
ter of a p.d of Butter & warm up with
some milk & mix up your spunge & lay
to rise before the fire roll it out in th
cakes, bake it in a slow oven, you mus
put a little salt in your flour, but not m
rise them before the ~~oven~~ fire before y
put them in the oven. ____

To Make Ratafia Cakes

Take 8 oz: of apricot kernels, if they cannot
be had bitter Almonds will do as well. blanch
them & beat them very fine with a little
orrange flower fwater, mix them with the
whites of three eggs well beaten & put to them
two pounds of single refin'd Sugar finely beaten
& sifted, work all together and it will be like
a paste, then lay it in little thins plates round
its on tin plates flower'd, set them in an oven
that is not very hot & they will puff up & be
soon be baked. _____

Sugar Vinegar

To 12 gallons of water add 14 p:d of Sugar,
put the whole of the sugar into six gallons
the water, boil it and skim it as long as there
is any scum rises, then pour it boiling hot over
the Vessel & fill it up with the other six gal:
of cold water, when almost cold toast a slice
bread spread it over with yeast & put it into the
Vessel let it work two or three days, then bottle

a strong brown paper over the bung hole,
prick it full of holes, lay a tile over the i
then set the cask in the Sun or a warm pla
till sour, which will be in six weeks or two
Months. ——————————

To Pickle Mellons

Make a strong brine that will bear an Egg
then throw it scalding hot on the Mellons
let them lie in it two days then take
them out and cut them down the middle
take out the inside fill them up with
equal quantities of mustard seeds, Ginger
bruised, & sliced Garlick — then take the
best white wine vinegar and boil in it
a sufficient quantity of Cloves mace
pepper and nutmegs throough it on the
Mellons scalding hot 3 or 4 Days till they
look green — cover them close and keep them
for use — they must be coverd close
every time they are scalded

M.B. Cucumbers are done the same way

To Pickle Mushroom brown

Take the dirt off the mushrooms & stalks
& the red gills out of them, peel the flaps
wash them in vinegar, then put them into as
much vinegar as will cover them — stew th
till tender with all sorts of spice except
Cinnamon a little salt, some shalotts &
Anchovies — bottle them for Use ——

The Buttons must be rubbd with flannel

To preserve Currants.

Extract Juice from Currants as you do for
Jelly & to every pint of liquor put three
quarters of a p.d of Sugar when boild
so as to jelly, put into it as many pounds
of Currants stript from the stalks as you
had pints of liquor let them simmer a sh
time & then put them into the jars or
potes ——

Fricassee Turnips

Cut your turnips in dice, when boiled
and put a little cream to them thicken'd
with flour & add a little lump sugar
to your taste. ——— Mrs Dundas

A Receipt to Curry after the India
manner

Cut two chickens as for fricasseeing
wash them clean & put them in a
stew pan with as much water as
will cover them, with a large spoonful
of salt sprinkle them & let them
boil till tender covered close all the
time, skim them well; when boiled
enough take up the Chickens & put
the liquor of them in a pan, then
put half a pound of fresh butter
in the pan & brown it a little, put
to it two cloves of garlic & a large
onion sliced & let these all fry till

52.

brown often shaking the pan, then
put in Chickens & sprinkle over the
two or three spoonfuls of curry
powder, then cover them close & let
the Chickens do till brown frequently
shaking the Pan, then put in the
Liquor the Chickens were boiled in
& let all stew till tender, If acid
is agreeable squeeze the juice of a Lemon
or Orange in to it. ————

A Dish of rice to be boiled, &
served up by itself. —

Take half a pound of Rice wash
it clean in salt and water then put
into it two Quarts of boiling water
& boil it briskly for twenty minutes
then strain it through a cullender
& shake it into a Dish, but do not
touch it. ——

N B. Beef Veal Rabbits Fish &c. may
be Curried with or without Rice ——

Take a full ripe Cucumber,
[cu]t it down the middle and take
[ou]t all the seeds, cut it in square
[p]ieces lay them in an earthen
[p]an, cover them over with salt,
[le]t them stand 24 hours, then
[w]ipe them quite dry, put them
[in] a pot with half a pint of
[w]hite-mustard Seed, 2 oz of long
[pe]pper, 2 oz of shallots, 1 oz of
[g]arlick, 1 oz of Roccombole, a
[la]rge piece of horse-radish sliced,
[6] Bay leaves, half a dz cloves
[o]r 4 blades of mace, & a little
[gin]ger. Then boil Vinegar enough
[to] cover them & pour on them
[co]ver them close & let them
[st]and 24 hours, then boil
[th]e Vinegar as before do so
[. . .] times the last

put all your pieces in &
them boil up 5 minutes &
then put them into your
Pickle pot cover it up till
the next day, then tye them
close for use.————————

India Pickel.

Take white Cabbage or Cauliflower, cut
in quarters, & boil them one minute,
put a little salt in the water then seperat
them leaf from leaf on a tin to dry them,
put them into the following pickel.

a gallon of vinegar one oz: of long pepp
½ lb of ginger, an oz: of Jamaica pe
half a pint of mustard seed bruised, a
of Termeric & a lb of garlick boiled
salted & dried as the cabbage, cover your
pickels boiling & let it stands to be cold
before you put in the cabbage. Any thing
else may be done in the same manner

To Candy angelica

When your angelica is young, cut it in lengths
boil it in salt & water till it is tender & green
dry it in clothes, & to every p:d of sugar chalks
put one p:d of fine sugar, lay your chalks
in an earthen pan, pound ye sugar & strew
it over them, then let them stand two days,
after which boil them till they are ~~tender~~
clear & strain them from your syrup,
beat another p:d of sugar very fine, & strew
it on your angelica lay it on plates to dry.
& put it into your oven after the pies
are drawn, turning them frequently on
clean plates ~~till~~ N:B If you find it difficult to preserve them green, when it
boiling make use of vine leaves. ————

Resoles

Take a p:d of veal which has been roasted
a little suet, a qr: of a p:d of butter & a little
lemon peel, chop all these together very fine
& then beat them in a mortar, add a little
pickels to your taste, & a little very good cream
fry your resoles in mutton suet what shape you

like beef. but minced veal is very good &
in the same way mixed as above. —

Lemon Pickle

One Doz: of lemon pickel the out rind or
grated very fine off, cut them into four
quarters leaving the bottom whole, then rub
upon them equally ½ a p.d of bay salt, & spread
them upon a large pewter dish, set them
into the sun to dry gradually until all the
juice is dried into the peel, after which put
your lemons into a pitcher with an oz: of
mace, half an oz: of cloves beat fine, 1 oz:
of nutmegs cut into thin pieces, four oz: of
garlic
peeled, & half a pint of mustard seed bruised
a little, tie all these together in a muslin
rag & pour two quarts of white wine vinegar
upon them. close your pitcher well up, &
let it stand for six days by the fire shaking
it up sometimes then tie it up for three, to
take off the bitterness, when you bottle it put
your lemons & liquor into a hair sieve press
them to get out the liquor & let it stand

another day then pour off the fine &
bottle it let the other stand a day or two till it
has refined itself so till the whole is bottled —

N.B. You may add your one quart of ve vinegar to the ingredients & let it stand a month
or two & it will be equally good. This pickle
is much better for being a longer time upon
the lemons than the receipt says, & will
keep for years.

To candy Angelica

When your Angelica is young ~~& tender~~
cut it in lengths, boil it in salt & water till
it is quite tender & green, dry it in clothes, &
to every p.d of stalks put one p.d of fine sugar,
lay y.r stalks in an earthen pan pound the
sugar & strew over them, then let them stand
two days, after which boil them till they are
clear & strain them from y.r syrup, beat
another p.d of sugar very fine & strew over your Angelica
lay it on plates to dry, & put them into your oven
after your pies are drawn turning them constantly
on clean plates. — N.B. If you find it difficult to
preserve them green, when it is boiling use vine leaves

58

M. Davison's receipt to pickle Pork
or Beef

To four Gallons of water put a p.^t
of course sugar two oz: of salt petre, & six p.^d
Bay salt into a large pan & let it boil, being
careful to take off the scum as it rises, when
no more scum rises take ye pan off ye fire
& let it stand to cool then put your meat in
the vessel where it is to remain & pour ye pic...
over it till all is cover'd —

N.B. Beef & Mutton will roast after being
the pickle a day or two, & pork is excellent.
Remember to wash the meat well before y.^u
use it ————

To dress a Breast of Mutton —
Boil your breast of mutton 'till the bones w...
... out, take off the skin & rub the meat o...
... yolk of egg, a few sweet herbs, parsley, onion
... crumbs of bread, with pepper & salt chopped
altogether & strewed over the meat, put it in a
dutch oven before a fire to brown, dish it up
with a rich gravy. —

India Pickles

Take half a p.d of ginger put it in water one
night, scrape it & cut it in thin slices put it
in a bowl with dry salt & let it stand till
our other ingredients are fit. Take half a p.d
of garlic, peel & cut it in pieces put it in
dry salt three days then wash it and put it
in the sun to dry. Take a q.r of a p.d of mustard
seed bruised very fine; an oz: of Turmrick, a
gallon of the strongest vinegar, put these
ingredients into a stone jar, let it be three
parts full. Take white Cabbage & quarter it
keep it in dry salt three days then dry it in
the sun. So do Cauliflowers Cucumbers, Mellons
Peaches, plums, Apples or any thing you .....
... Radishes may be done the same way
leaving on the young tops, also french beans
& asparagus the three last are to be salted
two days & dried as the others. You need not
empty your jar, but as things come in ....
put them in and fill it up with fresh vinegar
the more every thing is dried in the oven the
crimper it will be in the pickle, if the pickle
are not high colour'd enough, add as little

60 more termirie which makes it the colour
the india mango. never put red Cabbage
or Walnuts ~~because~~ because they spoil &
discolour all the rest

Biscuits — Mrs Dundas

Take two oz: of lard or butter, & two lb of
of flour, mix them well together stiff with a
little cold water, work or knead them very we
roll your biscuits very thin, & prick them ex
ceedingly, bake them on tins in a very quick
oven, looking constantly at them or they wi
scorch _____

Orange or Lemon Juice
& three pd of sugar (fine lumps) but one
quart of juice let it stand ten days, then
be the scum quite clear off, run it through
jelly bag & bottle it for use — do not cork
your bottles, but put a piece of paper over
the mouth. _____

Bolton Bunns

Rub a quarter of a p:d of Butter into 2 p:d
of flour, a q:r of a p:d of sugar, a handful of
Currants, two spoonfuls of good yeast, sett
to rise before the fire the yolks of two Eggs
and about a pint of warm milk, wet it
into a limp paste; & make it into fork buns

An excellent fish sauce — Mrs Howle
a quarter
Take a pint of Port wine, 12 anchovies, half
pint of vinegar, as much beaten pepper
as will lay on a half crown, two or three cloves
little mace, one nutmeg, a small onion
two bay leaves a little Thyme & parsley two
bits of radish put all this into a saucepan
and let it simmer till all the anchovies are
dissolved then strain it off & when cold
bottle it for use — It will keep 12 months
in a cool place — Melt your butter then
put in of this mixture to your palate

62

Mrs Fowle

Mock Turtle

Take a large calves head scald the off the h
boil it till the horn is tender, then cut it
into slices about the size of your finger, w
as little lean as possible: have ready near
pints of good mutton or veal broth
put to it half a pint of Madeira wine,
half a tea spoonful of Chyan pepper, a la
Onion, & the peel of a Lemon chopt very
a quarter of a pint of Oysters chopt, & the
liquor, a little salt, the juices of two large
lemons, some sweet herbs, & the brains chop
stew all these together about an hour, & se
it to table with force'd meat balls made
small, & the Yolks of hard Eggs ————

To dry Mushrooms

Take a peck of Mushrooms without taking
out the combs, peel the biggest & wash
the others, then put them into a kettle with
2 Onions, two handfuls of Salt, a good quantity
of pepper, cloves, mace, nutmeg, & some bay
leaves, then hang them on the fire, & let
them boil till almost all the liquor is
consumed, often stirring them about, &
when they can boil no longer for fear of
burning, stir into them about half a p.d of
butter, & when they are cold pick them out
& lay them singly on earthen platters, &
set them into the oven as soon as you have
drawn your bread, & so do as often as you
bake till they are throughly dry, then beat
them into a powder, & put it up close in
a gallipot: a spoonful of this ~~liquor~~ powder
gives a rich taste to any made dish, & helps
to thicken the sauce

Potatoe Yeast

Boil Potatoes of the mealy kind till they are
quite soft, skin, & mash them, add as much
hot water as will make them the consisten
cy of yeast but not thicker, to every p.k
of Potatoes put two oz: of course sugar
or treacle & when just warm to every
p.k of Potatoes put two spoonfuls of
Yeast keep it warm till it has done
fermenting, & in 24 hours it may be
used, a p.k of Potatoes will make a
quart of Yeast. when made it will
keep three months, lay the bread
eight hours before you bake it. —

NB For present use it will do very
well if your potatoes are put to the Yeast
the night before, or even two or three
hours. —

Fish Sauce

Two anchovies simmer'd in a little
water 'till dissolved & a little horse
radish to be boiled with it two spoonful
of Elder vinegar three or four spoonful
of white wine, a little mushroom cat
and to be thicken'd with Butter & flour

A Harrico of Mutton

Cut a neck of mutton into steaks
flour them & fry them brown on each s
put into your stew pan a piece of Butter
& two spoonfuls of flour, & let is simm
together 'till it is of a light brown kee
it stirring all the time add to it som
good gravy & let it boil up, then you
your steaks, & turnips & carrots, & let
stew one hour pepper & salt it to your ta
& two spoonfuls of Catchup. ———
When done, if greasy mix some flour
with cold water and put in to it, but le
it only boil up once afterwards ———

Rasberry Vinegar

Put two quarts of large, fine Rasberries into
one quart of the best Vinegar, let it stand
3 days near a fire, clarify 2 p^ds of fine
Sugar, strain off the juice from the Rasber
ries, add the clarified Syrop & boil all
together 'till it is fine — When it is cold
put it into small Bottles & use it as you
would Orgeat, mix it with Water to your
taste —   Mrs Lefroy —

Orange Jelly

An oz: of Isinglass boiled in a pint of Water,
add to it the juice of four China Oranges
one Lemon, & one Seville Orange, boil it
again with a little of the Lemon Peel, &
some lump Sugar — Strain it through any
thing thin ——

68 Snow Cheese

Take to a pint of cream grate the Peel of
two Lemons & squeeze the juice of them in
it with sugar to your taste, whisk it up to
a consistency put it into a small lawn vessel
& let it [illegible] to drain twenty four hours
& then turn it into your dish & serve it
up with sweetmeats or what you like ——

Pink Vinegar

Two quarts of the best whitewine Vinegar
one pint of Port wine, four table spoonfuls of anchovy liquor, two table spoonfuls of Walnut Catchup, 30 or 40 shallots
two table spoonfuls of India Soy, 1 oz: of
Cayon pepper 1 oz: of Cochineal, add [illegible]
horse-radish, Lemon [illegible] peel & spice
to your taste. Boil it a quarter of an hour
strain it off, let it stand till the
next day then Bottle it. ——

To keep Mushrooms as fresh
gathered . . . .

Take midle sized mushrooms that are
pretty close, rub them with flannel,
& throw them into milk & water; & salt &
change your water after they have bin a little
time, then wash them well, put them into
a sauce pan with a very little water
& strew some salt over them, a little
whole pepper, mace and an Onion; let
them boil a quarter of an hour very
quick; then put them into a cullender
when they are drained spread them
a coarse Cloth, & cover them close till
they are cold having first prepared
as strong as will bear an egg with an
onion, & some whole pepper boild in
when it is cold, & the mushrooms also
many of them into a wide mouthed
as it will hold, then fill

7° up with brine taking the Onion out
cork the bottle as close as [you] possible
& set there in a Cellar with the corks
downwards. When you would use them
lay them in scalding water, & milk, cha[nge]
the water, & milk several times 'till
you think them fresh enough either t[o]
fricasee or to put into any made dish

　　　　　　To pickle Mushrooms brown:
take the dirt off the Mushrooms and the
gills; & stalks from out of them peel th[e]
flaps wash them in vinegar, then p[ut]
them into as much vinegar as will c[over]
them stew them 'till tender with all s[orts of]
spices except Cinnamon a little s[alt]
some shallots, & Anchovies, bottle them
for use

N.B. the buttons to be rubbed with
flannel – it is better to pour the vin[egar]
boiling on the spices instead of stewin[g]
them with the mushrooms –

To make an Orange Pudding

Take the yolks of 12 eggs well beaten
½ lb of loaf sugar pounded, three oz of
candied orange peel shred, three quarters
of a lb of fresh butter clarified — mix
all these together, & bake them in a
dish with puff paste under & over it,
the oven being moderately hot. it will
bake it in less than an hour ————

To make Cow heel soup

Make a strong gravy with a shin of beef
& ½ pr of Cow heels boild tender, then cut them
in pieces & take out the large bones, one hour
before dinner, season the gravy with knotted
Marjoram, savory & thyme, the green of onions,
parsley, & shalots, chopt fine of each a spoonful,
half a pint of Madeira or sherry, four large
spoonfuls of Walnut, & two of mushroom Catchup,
pepper, & salt to your taste — flour the feet &
put them in a stew pan with the gravy, &
before it is sent to table take a little of

72. the soup almost cold, the yolks of two eggs
a little flour beat well together in a sauce
pan then boil it up & put it to the soup
& then give it all one boil up —————

Vegetable Pie

Take as many vegetables as one is sea
Cabbage, Turnips, Carrots, Cucumbers, & th
fry them in Butter, when well fry'
drain, & season them with pepper &
& lay them in layers in your dish or c
cover them with a crust, have ready
good gravy to put into the pie when bo
    It must not be put into a very hot o

To pickel Lemons

Take six Lemons of the largest size, pr
them all overs slightly, cut across the Knob
and rub in some salt very thoroughly, lay
in a jar well cover'd with salt, in a w
place for near a fortnight, then take
from the salt, & quite cover them with ver

vinegar, take a bit of thin cloth the 73
size of the top of the jar; & put into it a
pint of white mustard seed, some sliced
ginger & horse radish — they will not be
fit for use under two months, & the
longer they are kept the better they are.

Receipt to make Lemon Pickle
Take six large Lemons or a Doz: small ones
pare them thick cut them into eighth half
quarters. One pound of salt, six large
Cloves of Garlic, two oz: of horse radish
sliced thin two quarts of the best vinegar
Nutmeg, Mace Cloves, & Cayenne pepper,
of each a quarter of an oz; two oz: of the
best flower of mustard; let it boil a
quarter of an hour, then set it by, & stir
it once or twice a day for a fortnight,
then strain it off, & bottle it for use —

Lady Williams

Very good white Sauce for boil'd Carp

Take half a p.d of beal, cut it into small pieces, &
it in a pint of water with an Onion, a blade of
Mace two Cloves, a few whole pepper corns, a litt
salt & Nutmeg, and a bundle of sweet herbs, till is
as rich as you would have it. — Strain it off, & pu
it into your sauce pan, add to it a piece of butt
as big as an egg worked up with flour, a tea c
full of Cream, a tea Cup of white wine, & half a t
cup of Elder Vinegar. Mrs Austen

To make Calves feet Jelly Mrs Lawrence
(Two are sufficient if not very small)
A set of Calves feet nicely cleaned, the skin not taken
off, chop the bones, & boil them slowly in two quarts
of water till it comes to one. The jelly must stand
till the next day when the fat must be all taken
off. Melt the jelly, & put into it the juice of three
lemons, & the peeling cut very thin, three ounces
of loaf sugar a pint of mountain wine, & the
whites of six eggs beat into a froth. Let it just
boil, & strain it through a flannel bag. ——

Garlic Vinegar

A pint of garlic picked & cleand — put it into a pint
of warm vinegar to stand three days — then
strain it off and bottle it for use ————
Mrs Broughton

To preserve fruit of any kind
Gather the fruit in a dry day — allow a qr. of a pd. of
brown Sugar to a pd. of fruit — put a layer of Sugar
the bottom of the jar then a layer of fruit,
till the jar is filled — tie a Bladder over the
mouth of the jar very tight, put it in a bath

76 till the Bladder is tight & rises up in the mid
take the jar out & let it stand till cold, & the
tie paper over the bladder — The sweetmea
will not keep long after the bladder is open'd —
therefore best to do it in small jars —
Barberries, & Rasberries require a very little
more Sugar than other fruit

Pudding

Of Bread, Suet, Apples, Currants, 6 oz: each —
5 oz: of Sugar 6 Eggs a little Ratifia — boil it
three hours in a Cup

Miss Susan Debary —

To make Curree Powder

Take of Termeric Root, & Galangal Root each ha
an oz: Best Cayenne Pepper a quarter of an oz: Let
Termeric & Galangal be reduced to a fine powder
separately, then mix them with the other articles &
keep for use. — N.B. Two oz: of Rice powder to be
mixed also with the other ingredients. —

Mrs Jane Fowle.

White Soup

Make your gravy of any kind of
meat, add to it the yolks of four Eggs
boiled hard & pounded very fine. 2 [oz]
of sweet Almond pounded, as much
cream as will make it of a good Colour

To make Fish Sauce.

Cap^n Austen

Take two Heads of Garlick, cutting each clove in
two; add 1 oz: of Cayenne Pepper, 2 spoonfuls of
Indian Soy, 2 oz: of walnut Ketchup or pickle,—
Put them in a Quart Bottle, & fill it with cold
Vinegar; Cork it close & shake it well — It is fit
[for] use in a month & will keep good for years.

Swiss Soup Meagre

Take four Cabbage Lettuces, 1 Endive, Sorrel
Spinnage, Cherville, Chives, Onions, Parsley, Beet
leaves, Cucumbers sliced, Peas, or Asparagus; let
all these ~~herbs~~ be cut fine & no stalks put in, then
put a quarter of a p:d of Butter in a stew pan,
shake over your herbs when they are in the Butter
a small ~~spo~~ spoonful of flour & let them stew some
then pour in a quart of boiling Water & let it stew
till near dinner time; then add the yolks of three
in a tea cup of Cream, & a Roll if you like it.
Broth is better than so much water if you have it
If you have not all the vegetables above mention
will be very good with what you have & a little Se
range juice if you like.———

To Make Orange Wine

Take ten Gall: of Water, 30 lbs of fine Lisbon Sugar
the Whites of 6 Eggs well beaten, boil it together
a quarters of an hour skimming it well, then
d the juice of 33 Seville Oranges (reserving
Peel of 24 of them to throw into the Barrel)
juice of 36 sweet Oranges & of fifteen Lemons
x all well together & boil it up again ——
en cold for working take a larger toast
ver it with good yeast & let it stand work for
— days & two nights, then tun it —— Tack it off
the end of four Months, since the Cask & replace
e Liquor with a Bottle of Brandy & three p:ds
Lump Sugar —— You may Bottle it towards the
d of the year —————— Mrs C: Fowle ——

Green Gooseberry Wine

To every pound of Gooseberries (gather'd
when green) picked & bruised, ↑that is topped & tailed↑ put one Quart
of Water, let it stand three days stirring it
twice every day — To every gallon of juice
when strained put three p:ds of loaf sugar —
Put it into a Barrel & add to every 20 quar:
of liquor one quart of Brandy & a little
Isinglass — Let it stand half a year & then
bottle it — Miss Thornhill —

To make Cheese Puddings
Of Cheshire or Glocester Cheese take one
p:d and quarter, pound it in a Mortar with
the yolks of three Eggs & the whites of one till it is
a paste — lay it on a Butter'd toast & brown
with a Salamander

Mrs Dundas

To make Hogs Puddings

To half a gallon of whole Oatmeal well picked
and boiled very tender in milk & water the day before you make your puddings put the following
ingredients: eight Eggs leaving out half the whites,
the rind of a large lemon grated; Penny-royal
& sage chopped very fine of each a large spoonful; two teaspoonfuls of Jamaica pepper, three
of common black pepper after it is pounded;
half a p.d of crumb of bread grated fine; salt to
your taste. It must be mixed well together &
cold milk added to it to make it about the
consistency of a rice pudding: strain the blood
into it til it is of as dark a colour as you like,
& must put in a considerable quantity of fat
from the Pig which must be previously cut
to pieces the size of a large nutmeg. When filled
and tied up, put them into a Bucket of water
& wash them clean from whence they should
be taken one by one and put into a kettle of
boiling water; make it boils up, and they must
not do so for an hour; you must be

82. to prick them as they rise in the water,
they will burst — take them out carefully
with a nice stick & lay them up on clean
The puddings are equally good without the
Blood, but they will be white instead of bla

To cure Bacon

Rub the Flitches over with Salt Petre, partic
ly observing to force some in where the Hocks
taken off, then take one p:d of coarse feeding
Sugar & as much common salt mixed well tog
strew it regularly over the flitches cover it ou
with common salt & press it down close wit
the hand, let it lay twenty four hours then
it well & add a little fresh salt, let it be rubbe
& changed every other day for a month & then
up in a chimney where a moderate wood fire
kept for three weeks, and it should afterwards be ke
in a Chest with dry straw.
The Salt Petre should be pounded very fine &
dryed by the fire — One p:d will be sufficient
a Pig weighing eleven stone reserving enough
to rub over the Chines — Mrs Craven

To Pickel Pork

Bone it & cut it in such pieces as will lie
not conveniently in a powdering Tub which
...t be large & sound to hold Brine, the narrower
...eeper the better it will keep the meat; rub
...ry piece with salt Petre & then take common
...t, rub it over & over it with Salt — Strew salt
the bottom of the Tub, lay the pieces in as close
...possible strewing salt round the sides of the Tub;
...the salt melts at the top put on more — The
...t should be pressed with a broad & heavy stone
...eep it under the Brine. —— It will keep two
...rs, or may be used in two Months ——————

Ginger Beer   Mrs Craven ——

...o Gallons of Water, two oz: of Cream of Tartar,
...o pounds of Lump Sugar, Two Lemons sliced,
... oz: of Ginger bruised. — Pour the water
...iling on the ingredients, then add two
...oonsful of good Yeast; when cold bottle
...in stone Bottles & tie down the Corks, it is
...t to drink in 48 hours. —— A little more
...ar is an improvement; the Corks are not so a...
...tied down, which saves trouble, & glass Bottles will
                                                  do ——

84

To make a Veal Soup

Mr. Fartley

[Ta]ke a Knuckle of Veal and a piece of Ham, put it
[ov]er the fire with as much water as will cover it,
[add] three or four Onions, a head of Cellery & sweet
[her]bs; when it boils skim it well — stew it four
[hou]rs, then take up the meat from the bone & all
Gristle — Take off the fat, strain it through a
[sie]ve, thicken it with a little flour or white bread
[&] a little Cream, rub it through a sieve — then
[put] it over the fire, & let it have a good boil up —
[ga]rnish your meat & gristle. —— — ———

To make Gravy or Glaze Do——   —
[Tak]e a fore shin of Beef cut it in pieces, & lay it in a
[ste]w pan with six large onions — Turnip Carrot, & two
[head]s of Cellery & sweet herbs — set it on a stove & draw out
[the] gravy, let it be brown & all dried up, then put water
[to i]t, skim it very well & let it boil till very good Gravy
[t]hen strain it through a sieve, & when it is cold take
[off] all the fat, & take any quantity you want, set it
[on] the side of the Stove without a Cover, & let it boil
[till] it is like glue — put it on any thing you wish to Glaze
[with] a paste brush ——

Fish Sauce — Mr Hartley

Eighteen spoonsful of Raisin Wine, 9 do of Wine
3 of Walnut Catchup or Walnut pickle, some Mace
a few Cloves & one Nutmeg cut into three pieces — three
large onions & six Anchovies — Let all these simmer
together over a slow fire an hour, then strain it
through a hair sieve & bottle it for use —

N.B: How to use the above —

Take half a p.? of Butter cut it into three slices, flour
them & put them into a sauce pan with six spoons
ful of the liquor; set it on the fire to melt, because
it does not oil — when quite melted add four sp.
ful of Cream & the yolks of two eggs, stir it & pour it
the boat — If it remain on the fire it will curdle
A little elder vinegar is an improvement —

Bread Sauce — Do

Put some bread crumbs into a pan with a small Onion
& a little Gravy, let it boil, then add a little Cream — take
out the Onion before you put it into the boat & add a
little salt to your taste

Veal Cake —— Mrs Dundas ——

Bone a fat breast of Veal, cut some slices of
[h]am, the yolks of six Eggs boiled hard or a hand
[fu]l of parsley chopped fine; cut your Veal into
[thr]ee pieces, put the fat piece at the bottom
[of a] Cake Tin, then season it with pepper salt
[th]e parsley Eggs & ~~[crossed out]~~ Ham between each
[la]yer, put the thinnest piece of Veal at the
[top], & a Coffee cup of Water over it Bake it
[thr]ee Hours in a quick Oven with the bones over
[—] when done take them off & lay a weight on
[you]r meat in a small plate — as it cools the
[we]ight must be heavier that the Cake may be
[m]ore & firm —— The Brisket of the Veal is the
[on]ly part used: ——

88

Gooseberry Cheese

Take some green gooseberys, put
them in a jar, set it in boiling
water, till they are soft, then put
them through a sieve, & to every
pound of pulp add a pound of
sugar — Let it boil ten minutes,
if it boil longer, it will spoil
the colour —

W.S Craven

good luck to your jamming

Toasted Cheese

Grate the Cheese & add to it one egg,
a teaspoonful of mustard, & a little bu...
send it up, on a toast or in paper tray...

Dryed Gooseberries Miss Sharpe

Take six lbs of ripe Gooseberries; put them
to a preserving Pan with two lbs of Loaf
sugar powdered & strewed amongst them —
& them simmer until they begin to shrivel
— ⟨t⟩hen strain them from the juice, lay them
Dishes & dry them upon a hot hearth, or in
cool Oven; taking care not to burn them.
The same Syrup will do another six pounds.

Noyeau

One ounce of the finest Apricot Kernels, one pound
Sugar Candy a small quantity of Cinnamon
& Coriander Seed powdered — Infuse them ⟨in a⟩
quart Bottle of the best Brandy ⟨⟩
⟨⟩ — keep it well corked for three weeks, shak⟨ing⟩
every day — After standing a few days dra⟨in⟩
⟨fi⟩lter it through a Jelly Bag —

9°

Cherry Brandy as a Liqueur

Put the Cherries into a Jar & set it in hot water
to draw out the juice (as you would for Currant
Jelly) press it through a Sieve, & to every Pint of
this juice, put three quarters of a pound of ve
fine Lump Sugar, boil it & skim it until it
is fine, when cold add a pint of Brandy to
every pint of juice — The Stones must be bro
& the Kernels put into the Bottles —

N.B. Bitter Almonds, or Apricot Kernels a
good in it —
                    Wm Craven

If Morella Cherries are very fine they prod
nearly half a pint of juice to a pound

Solid Custard

In a quart of Milk boil an oz: of Isinglass
until the latter is dissolved, then strain it
through a Sieve, let it stand a short time
add the yolks of five Eggs well beaten
mix them with the Milk & set it on the
until it is as thick as a rich Cream, boil

...tard, sweeten & put it into a Mould to 91
...pare it for the Table — A few Bitter Al:
...nds, or a Bay leaf will improve the flavour
...ry much — Mrs Sawbridge

is receipt used at
...donn Lodge To cure Bacon   Mrs Fowle

To a Pig weighing fourteen score ——— Rub the
Flitches well over with one pound of Salt Petre
finely powdered particularly observing to force
...me into where the hocks are taken off. —
...ke one pound of coarse feeding sugar &
...s much common salt mixed well together,
...rew it regularly over the Flitches, cover it
...er with common salt, pressing it close down
...ith the hand. Let it lay for five or six days
...serving as the salt melts to cover it with
...esh. Then rub it well & change the flitches
...ery Week for six weeks, keeping them still
...ered with salt. — Hang them in a Chimney
...here there is a moderate wood fire kept for
...ee weeks — It should afterwards be kept free
...m damp
N.B. It is found best to put the greatest part
...sugar & salt upon the Gammons —

To make Noyau

Two Quarts of common Gin, one pound of
Bitter Almonds blanched — Let these ingre=
dients stand in a Stone Jar closely
corked until the bitterness be quite extract
then add one pound & half of white Sugar
Candy; filter the whole together through blo=
ting paper — If not sufficiently clear, add
a little Isinglass — N.B: The Almonds do
very well for Puddings afterwards —

Mrs Jas Austen

Scotch Orange Marmalade / Miss Debary
Each lb of Oranges requires 1 lb & ½ of lump Sug
Quarter the Oranges, then take off the rind & ce
part of the white substance permit — Put the rin
into boiling water & boil them quickly for a
hour or half or two hours — Slice them as thin as
possible — Squeeze the pulp thro' a sieve, adding
little water to the dregs — Break the Sugar fine
put it in the pan, pour the pulp on it — Whe
dissolved add the rinds, then boil the whole for

...nty minutes — A little essence of Lemon 3
may be added before it is taken off the fire
in the proportion of a small tea spoonful to
...ssue Oranges —

Raised Crust — Mrs Austen

...o lb of Flour ½ lb Butter ... Lard — Put the
...tter & Lard into a little milk, on the fire as soon as it
...ins to melt, rub it into the flour, wet it with
...ne of the hot milk — Make the paste
...ry stiff & keep it warm whilst you work
...p —

Short Crust Mrs Hulbert

...lb of Flour a qr of a lb of white sugar a qr
...a lb of Butter rubbed in — To be wetted with
...ee eggs, leaving out one of the whites to wash
...e pies on the tops, shaking white sugar over
...em at the last. —

Short Crust Mrs Austen

... pd of Flour a quarter of a pd of Butter a qr
...a pd of Lard rubbed in & wetted of a
...oderate stiffness with hot water. —

Macaroni

Stew a quarter of a p.d of the pipe Macar-
in milk & water until it is tender, the
lay it upon the top of a sive to drain.
Put it into a stew pan with two large
spoonsful of grated parmesan cheese, a
quarter of a pint of Cream, a small piece
of Butter & some salt. Stew it gently 'till
the whole seems well done, then put it
into a dish, strew grated Parmesan Che
over it, & brown it with a Salamander
in a Dutch Oven — It may be done wi
gravy instead of Cream if prefered. —

Mock Oyster Sauce

Take half a pint of Cream, one blade of Mac
pounded or boiled with the Cream, thicken
it with butter rolled in flour, & add essence
of anchovies to your taste; about one spoon,

To prepare Rice for sweet dishes

Take a qr. of a pound of the best Carolina
Rice & wash it in several waters, rubbing the
rice between the hands 'till the water leaves
the Rice quite clear; then pick it clean
give it one boil in water, strain it
on a sieve, & when free from water put
it in a stew pan that will hold three pints,
add to it a pint of milk, a small piece
cinamon & lemon peel. When it has
boiled up put it on a very slow fire that
it may do gradually for if the fire is strong
the Rice will burn — it should not be
stirred with anything while doing. —
When the Rice is quite tender (which
will be in about half an hour & half) take
out the cinamon & lemon peel, & put in to
it a piece of butter about the size of a
walnut & a little sugar, work it well with
a wooden spoon; when nearly cold build
in your dish about three inches high
making it smooth outside, & not too thick

96 it may be filled with stewed app
custard or any other stewed fruit.

To stew the Apples. –

Peel and slice about 14 moderate siz
Apples, put into a stew pan a small pi
of butter some lemon peel & cinnamo
with the apples; set them over a slow
fire 'till quite done & of a reddish col
put some sugar to them, & put it into
the Rice, first taking out the cinnamo
& lemon peel, set it in the Oven for
ten minutes before sending to table.
For a change, whisk the whites of fo
eggs to a stiff froth, mix with it a
hundred sugar, put it over the app
& strew sugar over it, then put it in th
Oven & bake it of a very nice color; s
it up quick or the soufflé will fall

Croquets of Rice are prepared in th
same way, only using cream inste

the rice instead of Butter & one
well beaten — make them round
size of a croquet, or small apples,
bread crum them twice — Either
on bake them, strew sugar over
m & send up quite hot.

Ginger Beer fit to drink in 24 hours
a Gallons of Water. 2 oz: cream of Tartar
lb lump Sugar 2 lemons sliced, 2 oz Ginger
ised, pour the water boiling on the in
dients, then add 2 spoonfuls of good
st; when cold bottle it in stone bot
and tie the corks down. —

Apple Snow

e prepare a lb of apples, boil or steam
em until tender & put them on a
ainer to drain — Add six oz: of
e loaf sugar & two whites of eggs
hipt into a froth first by itself — Whip
the apples also separately then put

98 altogether & whisk it up for a [half?]
hour until it all looms like snow. —

Mrs Berry

Bread Puddings in cups —
Quarter of a lb of grated bread, quarter
lb of butter, quarter of a pint of milk
the butter to be warmed in the milk &
mixed first with the bread — add four
eggs well beaten, sugar to your taste
half a glass of white wine; baked in
cups well buttered.

Blacking

C. Denton Esq—

One quarter of a ℔ of Ivory Black—½ ℔
Molases or course brown sugar, one
table spoonfull of oil of vitriol—One
table spoonfull of sweet Oil—one pint
of Beer—two wine glases of vinegar
as much prusian blue as will lie
a six pence

For cleaning Silks & Gauzes
Mix well together 6 oz: of honey, 4 oz: of soft soap
until it becomes a kind of paste, then dissolve
it in half a pint of strong Whiskey or hollands
spread your handkerchiefs on a clean
Table & rub it well with a soft brush, when
it has sufficiently imbibed the mixture
rince it in several waters but be careful
neither to wring or squeese it, hang it up
to drop but not in the air, when half
dry shake it well & mangle or iron it
For Gauze, add a little honey or white
sugar in the last rinsing water.—

66

For the tooth ach

[Op]ium in the gross purified; an equal quantity of Camphor
[ma]ke it into a pill, being moistened with spirits of
[wi]ne, to the size proper for the tooth to receive it — If
[the] first does not give ease in the course of half an
[hou]r, apply a second in its room —

Wm. S. Terry

Aperient Mixture
Dr. Hartigan

[S]ulphate of Magnesia two oz:, Water one pint
half, Tincture of Senna one oz: Mix there to
[Dose] Take a table spoonful Tea Cup full more or
less occasionally as required ———

Bark Mixture   Dr. Hartigan

Take half an oz of coarsely powdered Bark, pour
[up]on it half a pint of Boiling water — Let it stand
[th]ree Hours, pour it off & add half an oz of
[Car]damum Tincture, & two Spoonful of Elixir
[of] Vitriol — A Table spoonful to be taken three
[tim]es in a day ———

001

...mmine Powder & flannel to clear Gill...
...the dead Gold —

Milk of Roses / Cap.n Austen

½ Pint of Rose Water — ½ an oz. of Oil of
Sweet Almonds — 12 Grains of salt of Tartar &
be mixed well altogether.

Cold Cream   L.a Bridges
4½ Grains of white Wax, 1 Dm ½ Spermaceti
2 oz. of Oil of sweet Almonds, mixt well togr
& beat up with Rose water to a fine Cream

Black Draught   Mrs E. Knight
One oz of Senna & ½ do. of Epsom Salts ¼ of an
Manna ¼ of oz. of Cloves — The whole to be boil
ten minutes and to be divided into three
to each dose add a desert spoonful of Brand

Saline draft
Dissolve 26 grains of carbonate of Soda in
three table spoonfuls of Camphor Julep, add a
table spoonful of Lemon juice, a little sug
& drink it whilst in a state of fermenta
or not as most agreeable. Mr Jenkins. 18—

[...]aundar, & one hundred & twenty drops of
[...]incture of Castor. A small wine glass fo[r]
[...]dose. Rub the Camphire with a little
[...]randy, or Spirit of wine. —

Miss Delany. —

The Black Plaister

[...]ake of the best Oyl one pint, of the best
[...]d lead half a p:d of the best white lead a
[...]arter of a p:d, boil these for a while con:
[...]nually stirring it: then add two oz of the
[...]t Bee's wax, & then boil it again till it
[...] very brown, then rub a board with a
[...]th a little Oyl & let it cool & so rub it on
[...] board & make it up in Rolls for use

If you design it for searcloths add
[...]it one oz: of Castile Soap —

Mrs Raymond

Dr. Twiston's receipt for a Cold

Take volatile salt of Armonia 32 Grs. – Salt
petre 40 Grs. rub them on a Marble Mortar to
a fine powder, then add one oz: of Syrup of
Balsam & one oz: of oyl of sweet Almonds, an
six oz: of pump Water. The whole of the abo
will make four draughts, one of which shou
be taken three times in 24 hours, & to the nig
one add one Dram of Elixir of Parægorie:—

To Whiten Silk Stockings

When they are washed take a table or stoo
turn it bottom upwards, then make it close
with a sheet, pin the stockings round the
side, take a chaffing dish with Charcoal
break stone brimstone & strew over it, th
cover it close & it will make them white

To make Camphire Julep.

One Dram of Camphire, add a pint of Boi
Water, then put a qr. of an Oz. of Spirit of

For a Fever

grains of Tartar Emetic in an oz of water - a
salt spoonful to be given to a Child every two
hours till it operates or till all is taken, the
child who takes this quantity should be not
less than three years old.

Pot-powri

Gather your Roses free from wet & dry them
in a shady Room, & Lavender when quite ripe
the same. When they are perfectly dry they
must be put into a Jar with a quarter or half
lb: of orris powder according to the quantity
of Roses. Half an oz: of Benjamin & half an oz:
of storax, some Cloves pounded, some Cinnamon
over it ~~stitchedly~~ stir it now & then —
put any perfume you like on a bit of cotton, &
when dry put it with the rest into sweet Bags.

Soap for the Hands

Take of soft soap one p.d Spermaceti three
ounces. dissolve in a water bath — add
Camphor in powder one ounce — mix by
stirring it well together —

A Wash for Rooms

2 oz: of Indigo well ground
7 p.ds of London Whiting
1 lb of Glue

Boil the Glue in 9 pints of Water as a size,
then add your other ingredients to it, which should
be ~~used~~ cold & if made some days previously
it is the better — To wash the Rooms Baffins ta
of Blue, substitute dutch Pink & Spruce Ocre
N.B: If done upon Wainscoat the size to be rather
stronger of the Glue

days put your Pomatum into a Kettle
d water - Put this on the fire & let it
mmer for three hours then squeeze
much as possible from the bone
aves, thro a fine piece of Cloth ~~take~~
~~cake~~ putting it into a wide pan,
hen quite cold take off the cake &
row away the liquor, continue to melt
in the same way till all the liquor
seperated from the Pomatum –
ut it into Pots and keep it at least
~~ee~~ four months, it will be still better
the end of six months, in order to make
e Pomatum of a proper consistency
t will be necessary to add when melting
sufficient quantity of Mutton suet
e quantity of Suet must be regulated
the time of year it is to be used in

Tincture of Guiacum

2 oz of Powder of Guaiacum in a
int of Brandy to stand till it is clear

table spoonfuls is an oz —

The Camphor being a resin, never
thoroughly disolves pounding it &
rubbing it in two or three spoonfuls
of Brandy is the best method — it
may be obtained or not as most agree
able —

Rose Pomatum

Take a sufficient quantity of Lard of
the best kind put it into a deep pan and
stir in with a wooden spoon a quantity of
Rose leaves putting in a few at a time
cover it over with a Cloth and let it stand
all night — for ten days keep adding Rose
leaves putting in the yellow that is in
the centre of the flower, the first day
put a sufficient quantity of salt in to
keep the Lard sweet & at the end of ten

iting of the dog. Apply some of the ingredients
from which the ~~ingredients from which the~~
liquor was strained. to the bitten place.

Steel Pills

Take of Myrrh one Dram of Salt of steel
~~wormwood~~ half a Dram of Salt of Steel
twelve grains rub them together into
fine powder, then add two spoonfuls
of Nutmeg water, three Drams of Sugar
half a pint of Spring water ———
three table spoonfuls to be taken
twice in a day ——— It is better to
be made up into Pills ———————

Camphor Julep

Rub one Dram of Camphor with three
or four spoonfuls of Brandy, add two Drams
of Sugar, of one pint of boiling water, to
one oz: of a half of the Julep add a tea
spoonful of spirit of Lavender — two large

Cold Cream

A Dram of Spermaceti — A Dram of white
wax — two Oz: of oyl of Sweet Almonds —
Oz, & half of Rose water _____

Rose Pomatum

To a p.d of roses finely pounded one p.
of Lard, mixed well together, & let stand
three days — A small quantity of white
wax, melt it altogether & keep it stir.
when it has boiled a few minutes str.
it into your pots. _____

For the cure of the Bite of a Mad Do

Take the leaves of Rue, picked from the sta
bruised, six ounces. garlick. picked from the
stalks bruised, Venice treacle & Mithridate.
and the scraping of pewter, of each four oun
boil all these over a slow fire, in two quarts
strong ale, till one pint be consumed; then stra
it, and keep it in a Bottle close stopped, and g
of, nine spoonfuls to man or woman Seven morn.
fasting, and six to a dog, which will not fail
to effect a cure, if given within nine days, afte

601

Mrs. Davison's

Daffy's Elixer

Senna two oz: Elicampane, Guiacum chips,
Liquirice of each one ounce — Coriander
Cardamum seeds bruised of each a quarter
an ounce — Raisons stoned a quarter of
pound ————

Infuse these ingredients in one quart
of best double distilled Anneseed-water for
a week, then add one quart of water, stir
it every day, & let it stand one week more,
then strain it through Muslin, & tis fit for
use ————

For Worms

Rheubarb Powder, Jalap, of each
6 grains, Calomel prepared 4
grains, mix them up with honey,
to be taken fasting — The above quantity is
one dose for a child 4 or five years old, & should
encreased in proportion to its age. Two or three days
between each dose ————

thrown at the bottom of the pot. — Then a lay[er]
of flowers & so continue one layer upon an[other]
— till all the flowers are in — The flower[s]
may be put in as they are fit so as salt is al[so]
thrown in with them, the ingredients shoul[d]
be stirred every day with a[ ] wooden spoons, &
when the jar is full the spices should be [put]
in & the whole stirred up. It does best whe[n]
put into a large jar with a good deal of sa[lt]
& the jar stopp'd close for two or three mont[hs]
Then put more salt & stir it up well ——

Coral Tooth Powder

Prepar'd Coral — powder'd.
Kuttle Fish Bone, powdered, of ea[ch]
one ounce
Rose Pink three drachms
Powder'd Cassia Bark 2 drachms
Put all these together in a morta[r]
——

Varnish for Tables

...th pennyworth of alkenet root two ditto of
rose pink, & one pint of cold drawn Lintseed
Oyl. —

Lavender Water

To one quart of the best rectified spirits
of wine, put three quarters of an oz: of Essence
of Lavender & half a scruple of amber gris; shake
it together & it is fit for use in a few days —

To make a sweet Pot

One pd. of Violets, ½ ℔ of roses, ¼ of Thyme
in bloom, 1½ of sweet marjoram ¼ of a ℔ of
small myrtle, 2 ℔ of Lavender, ½ of Rosemary
in bloom, ½ of of Balm, ½ of Bay leaves broke
into small pieces, ½ pd. of Pinks, 3 ℔ of Orange
flowers not picked a large quantity of nutmeg
oz: of Cinnamon, 1 oz: of white pepper; the yellow
rind of 4 or 5 lemons grated — The flowers
herbs must be picked clean from the stalks
leaves, & the pinks seperated from their
stems, the spices must be pounded not too
fine. — Then two large handfuls of salt

Drink walnut leave tea nine mornings after

For the Staggers

Cinnabar of antimony, two drams; Musk half.
dram. Gum assafœtida half an ounce, Valeri
Root in powder half an ounce; Winters Bark
in powder half an ozi. made into a ball wi

Honey——

A receipt for Sore eyes
Salve

Take 1 oz of Butter without Salt half an oz of
cire wax 2 drachms of prepared tutty 1 Scruple
Camphire one table spoonful of rose water
& this all simmer a few minutes and stir it
till Cold — bind it over the Eye going to bed and
wash next morning with tutty prepared and Elder
flower water ———— may butter is best ————

for a pain in the side

Take Honey, and wheat flour mix
them well together; the thickness of a salve
spread it upon leather. then drop it all
over with hartshorn and put it to the
side. it must be repeted once in 12 hours
till the pain is removed.

for worms
Take cold drawn linced oil. to an infant a
Tea spoon a child ya nap spoonful a grown person
table spoonful, mix it with treacle. take it 9
mornings

A Receipt for an Ague

Take 40 Grains of Salt of Tartar
30 Grains of Snake Root
30 Gr.s of Salt of Steel
½ an ounce of Bark

Mix them together & divide them
into three parts; take one part
in a glass of Port wine or Cyder
in an hour after the fit is off, &
the other in twelve hours after
each other. Repeat the same in
eight Days after. _____

A good salve for sore Lips

Take an oz: of Bee's-wax, put it into an oz: of good
salad oyl, melt it over the fire & colour it with
Alkany root; when it has boild & is of a fine
red, strain it and drop in three penny-worth
of Balsam of peru, then pour it into the bottom
of tea Cups that it may turn out in cakes. ____

Mrs Towle

To cure worms

Four drams of wallnut leaves dryed & finely
powdrd mix'd up with honey, divide this into
eight doses & take one of them Morning & night
for four days successively. The Morning after take
for a purge jallap & Rhubarb an equal quanti
twenty grains of each for a grown person, to
children in proportion. ____

To Cure wounds in Cattle

Three penny-worth of tincture of Myrrh, four
penny-worth of turpentine, three penny-worth
of spirits of wine. ____

Black for Shoes

One oz: of Gum Dragon dissolved in a
quart of small Beer wort, add 2 oz: of
Ivory Black, mix it well together, put in
a gill of Brandy & it is fit for use.

Eye Water

Two penny-worth of white Copperas, one o
of Lime. put, to be dissolved in a quart of
spring water. To be shaken when used.—

To make Hard Pomatum

One lb of Beef Suet, 1/2 lb. Mutton Suet
1lb 1/2 of Wax, melt them separately, but
then together when nearly cold, or oz: of
Spices, pour it into you mould when
almost cold.— The Suet when melted
must be laid in cold water for a week
changing it every day.———

To make Ink

Take 4 oz: of blue gauls, 2 oz: of green
Copperas 1 oz & half of gum Arabic, break
the gaulls, the gum & Copperas must be
beaten in a Mortar & put into a pint
of strong stale Beer, with a pint of small
Beer, put in a little double refin'd
Sugar, it must stand in a chimney
corner fourteen days & shaken two or
three times a day. —————————

A Cure for Mange in Horses
or Dogs

Liver of Antimony & Brimstone
powder'd & equal quantity in weight,
mix'd up with lard or Butter to a sufficient
consistancy to make into Balls, about
the size of a Wallnut; let one be given
every morning for three weeks or a month.

The person who makes them up should
rub their hands in flour to prevent its sticking

A certain cure for a swell'd
Neck. ——

The day the Moon is at full a
gentle dose of salts shou'd be taken, &
then the next day take 20 grains
of burnt spunge in honey, syrop, or
any thing that will mix it; every
morning fasting till the moon chan
then take another gentle dose of salts
leave off till the Moon is at full again
& so on for a considerable time ti
benefit is found. —— It is best to
buy the spunge at apothecaries Ha
& it must be kept very close & dry

An easy but certain remedy
for a consumption.
Two ounces of the expressed juice of
Horehound, mix'd with a pint of ne
milk, & sweeten'd with Honey. ——

For the Gravel

One oz: of Marsh Mallow roots, two oz: of
earl barley; put them into 3 pints of
water, and boil it to a quart: strain it
to a bowl upon an oz: of Gum-arabic,
sweeten it to your taste with honey.—
A glass of this to be taken morning &
evening. ————

Remedy for the Hooping Cough

Cut off the hair from the top of the head
as large as a crown piece. Take a piece
of brown paper of the same size: dip it
in rectified oyl of amber, and apply it
to the part for nine Mornings, dipping
the paper fresh every morning. If the
Cough is not remov'd try it again after
three or four days. ————

This medicine is some—times used
in rubbing it along the back bone.————

To cure wounds in battle

Three penny-worth of tincture of Myrrh, Four
penny-worth of turpentine, three penny-worth of
spirits of wine; mix'd all-together apply it to
the wound. _____

A certain cure for a swell'd Neck.

The day the Moon is at full a gentle dose
of Salts should be taken, & then the next d:
take 20 Grains of burnt spurge (in Honey
Syrop or any thing that will mix it) every Mo:
-ing fasting till the Moon changes,

An Easy but certain ~~remedy~~
remedy for a Consumption _____

Two ounces of the express juice of
Hore-hound, mix'd with a pint of Cow's Milk
and sweeten'd with honey. _____

Black for Shoes

One ounces of Gum Dragon dissolv'd in a
quart of small Beer wort: add 3 ounces of Ivory
Black. mix it well together, put in a dram
Brandy & its fit for Use. _____

To Make Rasberry Vinegar

Take ripe rasberries pick'd when quite dry – fill a
stone jar with them within 2 Inches of the top –
then pour upon them Vinegar sufficent to quite
cover them – tye the pot quite close with leather
let it stand 12 Days in a dry place. then take
off the buff scum, and pour off the liquor quite
clear, by draining the drugs through a cullender
to a pint of Juice add a pound of lump Sugar boil
it to a ~~half~~ ~~syrup~~ ~~syrup~~ Sirup, keeping it well
scum'd. when quite cold put it into bottles tying
over them a piece of linnen or pricked paper.

Dr: Molesworth rect for fevers, sore throats
or any small beverage. —— in ulcerated sore
throats two, spoonfuls of Brandy to one of Syrop
taken ~~twice~~ three or four times a day. ——

123

Reader's guide & annotated transcription

A guide to using the transcription

Digital technology affords the reader precise images of *Martha Lloyd's Household Book*, but additional information adds clarity and context to the work. What follows is an exact transcription of the manuscript, capturing all its annotations, misspellings, cancellations, repetitions and omissions. The text has been fully annotated to enhance the reader's understanding. The transcription creates a complete record of the historical artefact. It is provided to aid the reader in deciphering the handwriting as it sheds light on common household practices in the long eighteenth century.

Inevitably, some challenges emerged in the process of transcribing the handwriting into print. These style notes and any important concessions are listed below. In all cases, the exact manuscript entries can be read and enjoyed on the facsimile pages provided.

Style and concessions

—Recipes that continue from one page to another are transcribed as one continuous entry. This eliminates the need to interrupt a lengthy recipe with a subsequent page number.

—The opening of most recipes was not indented. Some were clearly indented; others were minimally indented. Rather than interpret the writer's intent, all recipes are transcribed without indentations.

—Recipe contributor names are preceded by a em dash to help the reader identify the source. These names were most often recorded near the recipe title, but some were written near or at the end of the recipe. Biographical information on the contributors and their connection to Martha Lloyd can be found following page 49.

—Occasionally, original text has been lost along the crumbling edges of the manuscript. Sometimes the writer omitted a key word in the recipe. In both such cases, additions have been made in square brackets using the most plausible period source.

—Because this is not a line-for-line transcription, words hyphenated at the ends of lines are transcribed as complete words. Hyphens that appear within a line of text are retained.

—Frequently, sentences or recipes end with dashes made in various lengths. These are transcribed as full points. Dashes within sentences are retained but transcribed in the consistent length of an em dash.

—In the case of duplicate or extremely similar entries, text annotations are made on only the first entry.

—In general, notations are made on the first occurrence of a term that might be unfamiliar and not repeated on subsequent references; however, readers may consult the glossary for any repeated terms found in the manuscript.

—Recipes are presented as historical artefacts and not suggested in their present form for modern use. Many culinary recipes contain obsolete preparation and preservation methods that are best left to experienced recipe adaptors and food historians. Many original recipes, both culinary and medicinal, contain ingredients now known to be toxic and are not advised for consumption or use.

—Numerous and varied abbreviations have been used in the original text. Rather than annotating each occurrence, the following table is provided.

—In abbreviations written with a full point or colon, the punctuation was originally placed directly below the superscript. Since this placement is not always possible in type, the punctuation is placed immediately after the superscript. For an example, see page 16 of the original manuscript. The first line of 'To make Lemon Cheesecakes' calls for half a pound of almonds. Compare the original abbreviation for pound with its transcribed counterpart.

Common abbreviations

&c.	et cetera
Cap^n. Cap^{tn}:	Captain
Do do	ditto
Doz: dz	dozen
D^r:	Doctor
D^{rm}	drachm or dram ($\frac{1}{8}$ oz)
Esqr	Esquire
Gal.	gallon
g^d	ground
G^{rs}:	grains ($\frac{1}{60}$ drachm)
H^{ry}	Henry
L	*libra pondo* (pound by weight)
lb	pound
L^y.	Lady
M^r.	Master/Mister
M^{rs}.	Mistress/Missus
NB NB. N.B. N.B: N:B:	*nota bene* (note well)
Oz: oz: oz	ounce
p^d p^d. p^d: p^{ds}:	pound(s)
p^r.	pair
q^r q^r. q^r:	quarter
q^t.	quart
ye y^e y$^{\underline{e}}$	the
y^r y^r:	your

71

Martha Lloyd's Household Book

[catalogue code] CHWJA: JAHB34[1]

[doodles; letter *L*]
Cookery interest
Lloyd

I

A Pease Soup

Take two quarts of pease boil them down to a pulp strain them, put half a p^d of Butter into a stew pan, Sallery, half an Onion, & stew them till tender. Then put two anchovies, pounded peper, Salt, mint and pasly each a small handful, & Spinach & beat of each a small Quantity half a spoonful of Sugar. The Soup to be boiled as thick as you like it and the Whole to be to-gether boiled up & Dished.

---

1. Reference number for Jane Austen's House international cataloguing system. CHW [Chawton] JA [Jane Austen]: JAH [Jane Austen's House] B [book] 34 [unique number assigned to this item in the collection].

To Make light Wigs[2]

Take a pᵈ & half of flour & half a pint of Milk Made Warm, mix these to-gether, and [cover it up,][3] let it stand by the fire half an hour, then take half a pᵈ of Butter and half a pᵈ of sugar and work these in the paste and make it into Wigs with as little flour as possible; let the oven [be pretty quick] & they will rise very much.[4]

2

A pound Cake

Take a pound of fine flour well dried,[5] then take a pound of Butter, & work it very well with your hands, till it is Soft, then work into it half a pᵈ of gᵈ Sugar, then beat 12 eggs puting a way half the Whites,[6] then work them also into your Butter and Sugar, then strew your flour into your Butter Sugar, & eggs, by little & little, till all be in, then Strew in 2 oz: of Carraway Seeds, butter your pan, and bake it in a quick Oven,—an hour & half will bake it.

[Pages 3 and 4 are missing from the manuscript, but their contents are listed in the index:

A Plumb Cake—3
A White Custard—4
A rice pudding—ibid]

5

---

2. Light, fluffy buns made with milk or cream, often with seeds such as caraway.
3. Insertions from Hannah Glasse, *The Art of Cookery Made Plain and Easy*, 1748, p. 288.
4. The critical last line of Glasse's recipe was omitted: 'Mind to mix a quarter of a Pint of good Ale-Yeast in the Milk.'
5. A practice required to remove dampness caused by the weather and the cooking environment.
6. Six whole eggs plus six egg yolks.

Wallnut Catchup[7]

Take green Wallnuts[8] and pound them to a paste then put to
every hundred two quarts of Vinegar with a handful of Salt put it
altogether in an ~~handful~~ earthen pan keeping it stirring for eight
days. Then Squeese it through a coarse Cloth, & put it into a well
tind Sause-pan,[9] when it begins to boil skim it as long as any scum
rises and add to it some Cloves, mace, sliced ginger, sliced nutmug,
jamaica pepper corns, sliced horse radish, with, a a few shalots, let
this have one boil up, then pour it into an earthen pan, and after it is
cold bottle it up, dividing the ingredients equally into each bottle.

6

A Pease Soup

Take five or six Cucumbers pared and sliced the white part of as
many Coss Lettice[10] a sprig or two of Mint; two or three Onions,
some pepper a little salt a full pint of young Pease[11] a little Parsley
half a pound of butter put them altogether in a sauce pan to stew in
their own liquor for an hour and half or till they are quite tender;
then boil as many old Pease[12] pulp them through a cullender[13] and
mix them in a quart of the liquor or more as you like it for thickness
when the herbs are stewed enough put them in and serve it up.

---

7. A thick condiment sauce. Unlike modern ketchup, eighteenth-century ketchups
were not tomato-based.

8. Walnuts picked in the spring before they are fully mature, when the green skin
is pliable and the inner nut soft.

9. A copper saucepan lined with tin to prevent a toxic reaction between certain
ingredients (e.g. vinegar) and the pan metal.

10. Cos lettuce is named for the Greek island of Kos where the lettuce is said to
originate. Known today as romaine lettuce, other eighteenth-century names include
Manchester lettuce and Roman lettuce. The variety is characterized by crisp leaves
and a white heart.

11. Early cookbook writer Charlotte Mason notes that tender young peas require
minimal cooking: 'young pease half-boiled'. With mature peas (ideal for drying), she
instructs the cook to 'boil them till tender'. Charlotte Mason, *The Lady's Assistant for
Regulating and Supplying the Table*, 1787, p. 194.

12. Dried peas.

13. Variant spelling of colander.

A receipt for a Pudding[14]

If the Vicar you treat,
You must give him to eat,
A pudding to hit his affection;
And to make his repast,
By the canon of taste,
Be the present receipt your direction.

first take two pounds of Bread,
Be the crumb only weigh'd,
For crust the good house-wife refuses;
The proportion you'll guess,
May be made more or less,
To the size that each family chuses.

Then its sweetness to make
Some currants you take
And Sugar of each half a pound
Be not Butter forgot
And the quantity sought
Must the same with your currants be found

Cloves & Mace you will want,
With rose water I grant,
And more savory things if well chosen;
Then to bind each ingredient,
You'll find it expedient,
Of Eggs to put in half a dozen.

---

14. Because of its good-humoured and intelligent tone, this verse is attributed to Mrs George Austen. It is thought to have been written specifically for Martha and intended for inclusion in her household book. (*Jane Austen: Collected Poems and Verse of the Austen Family*, pp. 32–3.)

Some milk dont refuse it,
But boiled ere you use it,
A proper hint this for its maker;
And the ~~whle~~ whole when compleat;
In a pan clean and neat,
With care recommend to the baker.

9

In praise of this pudding,
I vouch it a good one,
Or should you suspect a fond word;
To every Guest,
Perhaps it is best,
Two puddings should smoke on the board.

Two puddings!—yet—no,
For if one will do,
The other comes in out of season;
And these lines but obey,
Nor can any-one say,
That this pudding's with-out rhyme or reason

10

To make Hams

at Portsdown Lodge[15] half the quantity of Sugar and rather more Salt
than the Receipt states [annotation]

Take Two legs of Pork, each leg weighing about 15 pounds, rub them
well over with two oz: of Salt petre[16] finely beaten, let them lie a day

---

15. The second home of Admiral Sir Francis Austen, brother of Jane Austen.
Martha and Frank married in July of 1828 and purchased the house around June
1830. Portsdown Lodge was located near Portsmouth, the home of the Royal Navy.
The notation appears to be a later addition to the recipe.
16. Saltpetre, or potassium nitrate, is a naturally occurring chemical compound
used in food preservation. When used to cure meats, it reacts with haemoglobin to
create a pink colour.

and night then take two pound of Brown Sugar,[17] one pound & half of common Salt,[18] mix them together and rub your Hams with it, let them lie three Weeks turn and rub them in the pickle every day.

Calves feet Jelly[19]

Take a set of Calves feet boil them to a Strong Jelly. the whites of 16 eggs five Oranges & two Lemons a Stick of Cinnamon two bay leaves & a sprig of Rosemary sweeten it to your taste if you cannot get oranges put five Lemons pare the peels in some of the Jelly boiling hot an hour before you make them.

A Carraway Cake

Take 3 p^d of flour, 2 p^d of Butter ~~rubbed~~ rubed into the flour an ounce & half of Carraway seeds 12 spoonfuls of Milk, 12 spoonfuls of Yeast, 12 yolks of eggs 4 whites, beat all these well to-gether put them into your flour stiring it very well, let it stand by the fire side a quarter of an hour to rise. when the oven is hot strew in the carraway's stiring it all the time, then butter your pan and put in your cake. an hour and half will bake it.

   NB Put in a pound of Sugar

To bake a buttock of Beef

To a Buttock of Beef of 18 pounds take 2 p^d of common Salt, half a p^d of coarse sugar, & two oz: of Salt petre let them be well rubbed in, and turn the Beef every day for a fortnight. then roll it up very

---

17. A natural sugar that retains a portion of the molasses from its original and partially evaporated sugar cane liquor. It is known today as brown or muscovado sugar.

18. Coarse salt or kitchen salt.

19. A sweetened citrus aspic congealed by the gelatin in the calves' feet.

tight with beggars tape;[20] put it into a deep pan and cover it with equal parts of red wine and water. bake it five hours take it out of the Liquor when it is cold. it will keep six or 8 weeks.

12

A very good way to dry Beef

Take eight ribs of Beef, lay it on a stone or board, & rub a little Salt upon it let it lie three days, then rub well into it 2 oz: of Salt petre made hot at the fire, let it lie ten days turning it once in two days, and put a little Salt to it as you see it wanting then hang it to ~~dry in to~~ dry in the Kitchen, but not too near the fire. when dry keep it in Malt.[21]

Fish Sause[22]

Crawfish shells pounded in a stone mortar put some thin gravy[23] to them, a bit of Cinnamon & a bit of crust of Bread, stew this altogether till tis strong, then strain it off, and mix it with Butter and anchovey, lobster shells will do as well as Crawfish.

13

Blanch Mange

Take half an oz: of Bitter Almonds, blanch them & pound them very fine, then put them into half a pint of good Cream with Sugar then

---

20. Thin strips of woven fabric, probably cotton, used to secure meats in a compact shape. Compares with today's butcher's twine or kitchen string. A similar recipe for 'Rump of Beef A-la-mode' instructs the cook to 'skewer it and bind it with tape.' (Mason, *The Lady's Assistant*, pp. 123–4.)

21. The germinated and dried form of grain, most commonly barley when used in brewing and distilling. Most cooks would have a ready supply of malt for making the household beer and ale. Malt was also pounded and used as flour. It is unclear whether the cook was to store the dried beef directly in the malted barley or in flour.

22. A popular condiment, most often fermented, for use on fish, seafood or meats. Mixed with butter, it made a flavourful addition to cooked vegetables.

23. Cooking stock or broth.

take half an oz: of Isinglass,[24] & put boiling upon it, half a pint of new milk let it stand to be cold then put it altogether, boil it about 3 Minutes, keep it stirring all the while, then strain it into something. keep it stirring till cold. then put it into cups, which must be wetted that they may turn out easily.

New College Puddings[25]

To make a dozen of new College puddings take two pounds of grated bread, half a pound of Beef Suet[26] minced very fine, half a pound of Currants 3 eggs a quarter of apound of Sugar a little Nutmeg, one spoonful of rose or orange flour water; mix them all well together then clarify half a pound of Butter, put them into it & set them over a gentle fire keep them ~~stirring~~ turning as you find them get brown they will be done in about 20 minutes serve them up in butter; or wine & Butter.

14

To Make Mead[27]

To every Gallon of Water, put four pound of honey, & for 20 Gallons add as follows, two oz: of Nutmeg, half an oz: of Mace half an oz: of Cloves 2 oz: of Race-Ginger,[28] all just bruised, and sewed up in a ~~Lining bag~~ Linen bag;[29] then add a large handful of Sweet briar with the above. boil all-together one hour Skiming it all the time it boils;

---

24. A powdery gelling agent made from fish bladders that have been dried and pounded. Compares with today's gelatin.

25. These puddings are divided into small portions and fried in butter as opposed to being boiled in a cloth like many traditional puddings.

26. The hard fat located around the kidneys and loins of beef and mutton, used raw. Suet was a staple ingredient in both sweet and savoury puddings.

27. A fermented beverage of ancient origin, made from honey.

28. Race or root ginger was used fresh in both sweet and savoury dishes. The pounded yellow flesh added a sweetly pungent taste. The dried powdered root was also used in eighteenth-century cooking to provide a more fiery taste.

29. A spice bag, also of muslin, that allowed flavours to infuse the beverage without leaving particles behind.

then strain it off as you do Wort,[30] add a little Barm[31] to it, if it does
not Work[32] tun[33] it and let it stand a day or two, then add the juice of
6 good Lemons, with the rind of them and your bag of Spices in the
barrel stop it up close for 10 or 12 Months then bottle it for use. you
may add more spices if you like it.

15

To make Turtle[34]

Take a Calves head, dress it as you do the feet. let it lay in cold
water for some time, then boil it in a Cloth very tender, then cut it
into small pieces, make your gravy of veal and beef minced very
small, put it into a jar with a little sweet herbs, water, peper, & mace,
Chian,[35] Butter & onion, add your Gravy to your meat, & put in half
a pint of Maderia Wine,[36] 2 anchovies worked up in flour & butter,
to make it as thick as you like it, the yolks of 12 Eggs boil'd hard, the
brains made green with spinage, and beet root fryed.

The force meat balls[37] for the turtle. take the sweet bread[38] of the veal
or some Lamb cut into small pieces, with twice as much suet, & some
crumbs of bread, two eggs, salt, mace, Lemon peel. a little pepper, &
an an onion boiled, beat it all together for some time, then take the
yolks of 3 hard eggs, cut small, and put it to it; make it into large Balls
and fry them.

---

30. The liquid extracted after grains are mashed during the brewing process. The
wort contains sugars that feed the yeast and lead to fermentation, producing alcohol.
31. The yeasty scum or foam that forms on top of the brew.
32. That is, begin fermenting.
33. Put it into a cask or tun.
34. In this case, a mock turtle stew where a calf's head is substituted for turtle.
35. Cayenne, a moderately hot dried and powdered chili pepper.
36. A fortified wine from the Portuguese Madeira Islands. Madeira was an
alternative to French wines, which were heavily taxed during Britain's frequent wars
with France.
37. Sausage meat balls; from the French *farcir*, to stuff.
38. Sweetbreads is the general term for either the thymus (gullet, throat or neck
sweetbread) or the pancreas (belly, stomach or gut sweetbread) glands of calf or lamb.

To make Lemon Cheesecakes

Take ~~haff~~ half a p^d: of almonds blanch'd in cold water, let stand all
night, beat fine with Orange flower water[39] take half a p^d: of fine
sugar, then take the Peal of two Lemons paired very thin, boil it in
water till they are very tender & not bitter; then beat it very fine in
a Mortar.[40] with the sugar, then mix it with the Almonds, take eight
eggs leaving out half the whites;[41] take 3 q^r: of a p^d: of butter melted
& let it be cold, then mix it altogether bake it in fine paste[42] in small
patty pans put some sugar in your paste.

To Pot Beef

Take the lean of fat beef & lay it in Salt Petre 28 hours[43] then bake
it in an earthen pot with butter or fine shred beef Suet, when it is
baked, take ~~take~~ the gravy from it & ~~bake~~ break it in pieces with your
hands & season with pepper salt Cloves & Mace & Nutmeg then, put
it into the pot again & fill it up again as before & set it into the oven
and bake it again then put on it clarified butter; this will keep a year.

---

39. An aromatic flavouring distilled from fresh bitter-orange blossoms.
40. The work bowl of a mortar and pestle was often made of marble for culinary
use. They could also be made of wood, although less durable and prone to absorb oils
and other liquids.
41. Four whole eggs and four egg yolks.
42. Pastry crust, meaning shortcrust or piecrust pastry.
43. Several period sources specify a period of 'twenty-four hours'. This may be an
error made by the initial or a subsequent recorder.

To make Gingerbread

Take four Pints of flour rub into it 3 quarters of a p^d of butter 2 oz: of Ginger a Nutmeg, one oz: of Carraway seeds a quarter of a pint of Brandy 2 p^d: of treacle,[44] mix it altogether; & let it lay till it grows stiff then roll it out, & cut it into cakes, you may add what sweet-meats[45] you please.

To make Cabbage Pudding[46]

Take the lean of Venison or Veal chopt very small, put to it beef suet chopt small then take a piece of Cabbage half boiled chopted it & mix it with the meat, season it with pepper salt & nutmeg two yolks of eggs then take the Cabbage leaves & dip them into them boiling water & put your meat into them, the bigents bigness you would have them with thread they must boil two hours then serve them up with melted butter.

To make Orange Wine

Take 2 Gallons of Water let it boil an hour, when it is cold have ready a hundred & twelve p^d: of Malagoc Raisons[47] picked, & chopted small; when the water is quite cold put itn on the raisons let it stand a fortnight stirring it twice every day, then strain the liquor from the raisons squeeze them very hard, let the liquor run through a hair

---

44. Black treacle, like molasses, is formed during the sugar refining process when sugar cane juice has been boiled down.

45. Any confectionary variety of sweets such as candied fruits, caramelized nuts, bonbons, sugarplums or other candy.

46. Although puddings could be savoury or sweet, this recipe produces not the typical cloth-boiled pudding, but a dish similar to today's stuffed cabbage leaves.

47. Sun-dried raisins from the province of Málaga in Spain, with a dark red colour and an intensely sweet flavour. The quantity of 112 pounds is excessive and probably an error made in copying. Similar period recipes would suggest 7 to 8 lb of raisins for 2 gallons of water.

sive[48] then have ready a [omission] Civil Oranges[49] ~~upon~~ pare'd very thin squeeze the juice of the Oranges upon the Peels & put that and the liquor into the Vesel and when it has done working stop it up you may ~~stop it~~ bottle it when fine which will be in about two Months

18

Cowslip Wine

Take eight gallons of Water boil it and let it stand to be ~~cold~~ a little cool then put into it 8 Gallons of cowslip flowers picked and 8 lemons sliced, stir it together well and so do for 5 or 6 days then strain it out and add to this quantity a quarter of a L100[50] of Lisbon Sugar[51] stir it well together & spread a toast of brown bread with new yeast on both sides & put to it let it work as long as it stood before, & then turn it into a Vesel of the same size when fine draw it but not to soon.

To Make Currant Wine

Pick the Currants off the stems, and pound them, & to every gallon of ~~water~~ liquor put two quarts of spring water, & two p^d: of of Sugar Barrel it up watch it till it is clear (for all these wines must be taken just in the Nick of time) when they are first clear or else they are spoiled) bottle it out; if you would have it to drink soon you must put the less Sugar in it, in some weather it will not be clear in the Vesel till it has stood to Long for the body. so you must draw it of into bottles & in a week after decant it into other Bottles putting a lump of Sugar into every bottle.

19

---

48. A sieve formed from a wooden hoop with closely strung horsehair mesh. Here the sieve would catch the raisin flesh and tiny seeds, allowing the juice to pass through.

49. Tart, nubby-skinned oranges from Seville in Spain, available in the UK for a three-month period, generally December to February.

50. The L superscript may stand for *libra* as in the Latin *libra pondo*; *libra* meaning a Roman pound and *pondo* meaning 'by weight'.

51. Portugal produced the finest quality loaf sugar available. Many recipes dating from the mid-eighteenth century call for Lisbon sugar specifically.

To Pickel Saphire[52]

Take samphire & put it into a brass pot & to each peck[53] of Samphire
put in 2 quarts of ~~water~~ white wine Vinegar & on quart of water lay
something of weight to keep it under the water, & paste the pot lid
down close that no steam may come out let it not boil to long for
it will not be so well set it of the fire till it is cold, then put it in an
earthen jar & the same liquor to it, put no salt.

To Pickle y͏ᵉ Dutch Plum or White Dam[son][54]

To a Gallon of White wine Vinegar put 3 pints of Mustard 13 heads
of garlick a good handful of shellotts a good handful of horse-radish,
when it is sliced three races of Ginger sliced half an oz: of Jamaica
peper & what salt you think fit.

    The Plumbs must be gatherd before they are quite ~~fit~~ ripe, when
they are turning yellow. they must be cut a little on one side to let in
the liquor put them in raw, your Mustard must be made as to eat. You
may do Mellons or Cucumber the same way only take out the inside
and rub them with Salt.

20

To Pickle Onions

Take half a peck of the smallest Onions you can get, peal them and
put them into fair water & salt let them stand all Night then boil them
a little in fresh water & skim them very well make the pickle as for
Cucumbers, let the Onions & the pickle be cold when you put them
together it is the best way to still the Vinegar with the Spices in it.

---

52. Samphire, a succulent plant that grows wild and thrives in rocky, salt-sprayed
regions along the coast of the UK. Harvested in early spring, it can be eaten fresh or
pickled.

53. A unit of dry measure equivalent to one fourth of a bushel or 2 gallons.

54. A small plum-like native fruit, damsons are most commonly used in preserves
or jams due to their astringent quality and sour taste.

To Make Hartshorn Jelly.[55]

To four Oz: of hartshorn shavings, one quart of Water & boil it dry, then put another quart of water & boil it till it will Jelly, ye whites of two Eggs & beat them to a froth with the juice of a lemon & half an oz: of orange a stick of Cinnamon & sugar to your taste, run your Jelly through a bag[56] & let it stand to be a little cool before you put your eggs to it then boil it till it looks clear or the eggs begin to sink then run it through the bag till it is quite Clear.

21

To Make Fish Sauce for keeping

Take a pint of Port Wine, 12 Anchovies, a Qarter of a pint of Vinegar, as much beaten peper, as will lay on a half Crown;[57] 2 or 3 Cloves, & as much Mace; a Nutmeg, a small Onion, 2 bay leaves, a little Thyme, & parsley, 2 bits of horse radish; put it all-together in a Sauce pan, and let it simmer, till all the Anchovies are disolved; then strain it off, and when cold, bottle it up; it will keep half a year in a cool place. mix it with Melted butter, the quantity according to your taste.

To Make a rich thick Cheese

Take seven quarts of Cream, ten gallons of Milk, let them be cool run; then break it gently take off out the whey,[58] put it into a great

---

55. Obtained from the antlers of a male deer and used culinarily in either shaved or powdered form. The heat-activated hartshorn worked as a thickening agent with leavening properties similar to today's baking ammonia or baking powder.

56. A common practice to strain solids from liquids. Typical jelly bags would be made of canvas or muslin.

57. Based on the diameter of a late Georgian half-crown coin (32 mm or 1¼ inch), roughly ½ teaspoon of pepper.

58. The recipe is written assuming that the reader knows to separate the cream or milk with rennet or other coagulating enzyme, resulting in curds (solids) and whey (liquid).

85

thick Vate with a hoop[59] in it; lay the Curd gently into the Vate, lay a small weight on it, press it gently for an hour & half; then take it out, & slice it thin, put it into a tub of Cold water; let it lay a quarter of an Hour, then take it out & make it very dry with clean cloaths; then put in a pint of cream (it must be very thick) after it is broke in small pieces as big as a Wallnut, mix them, then put it gently into the Vate, lay a pound weight upon it, press it gently by degrees till night with more weight, then put it into the press: next morning turn it, salt it & put it into the press again; at night turn it & salt it a little more, put it into the press: next morning bind it about with fillets,[60] set it to dry quick, change the fillets daily.

22

To Make Wafers

Take eight eggs, leaving out half the whites[61] & mix them with a pint of skim Milk; make it into a thick batter, the same as for pancake, put in four or five spoonfuls of new yeast, a grated nutmeg, near half a p^d of Butter melted, beat it well to-gether, you may warm the Milk a little it will rise the better; [The remainder of this recipe was presumably on pages that are now missing from the manuscript.]

[Pages 23–26 are missing from the manuscript, but their contents are listed in the index:

A Lemon Pudding—23
To make Marmalade—24
Damson Cakes—
A fine Pancake—26
To Make Wigs—26]

---

59. A large wooden vat fitted with a wooden hoop; used to form the cheese.
60. A narrow piece of thin material, most likely a loose-woven cotton that would allow liquid to drain from the cheese. Compares with today's cheesecloth.
61. Four whole eggs plus four egg yolks.

To make a fine Cake

Take 2 pound of fine flour dried & sifted, a pound of butter rubing it into the flour, take 3 pound of currants wash'd ~~wash~~ & pick'd, and set in an oven to dry, then mix them in the flour after the butter, then take candid orrange peel[62] lemon-sittron[63] & Apricot of each ~~half~~ a quarter of a pound, a Nutmeg, & some ~~spice~~ mace, mix them together & four eggs but two whites,[64] beat the eggs well with two spoonfuls of sack,[65] & a pint of Yeast, & a pint of cream, boild & let stand to be cold, then strain them & make it into an indifferent stiff paste,[66] keep out some of the cream till you see how it is; let it stand an hour before the fire to rise, & when the oven is hot turn it into a hoop & work it with your hands, let the hoop be butter'd. Dont rub the butter to hard in the flour.

A Rice Pudding

Six ounces of rice flour, one quart of cream, mix it well together & boil it, put to it half a pound of butter, half a pound of sugar, & one nutmeg grated & then take it off, when cold beat six eggs whites & all & put to it butter your dish before you put it in. Bake it quick you may paste your dish[67] if you please.

---

62. Orange peel that has been boiled in sugar syrup then air-dried until crisp.
63. Citron, here the candied peel of the fruit.
64. Two whole eggs plus two egg yolks.
65. A fortified white wine from mainland Spain or the Canary Islands. Compares with today's sherry.
66. Dough that will hold its shape.
67. Line the dish with a pastry crust.

To make scotch Collops[68]

Take part of a leg of veal & cut it thin into what shapes you please hack it with the back of a knife[69] till it but just hangs together, fry it in fresh butter, put all into your pan cold.

For the Balls

Take double the quantity of suet you do of meat & beat it very small, season it with nutmeg salt pepper & anchovy to your taste, eggs according to the quantity of meat put crum of bread mix all well together & make them up some round & some long cut off the Udder of the veal & stuff it with the same as the balls truss it round & roast it, & lay it in the middle of the dish.

For the sauce

Take some bones or some meat put it in water with a bundle of sweet herbs as Thyme Margrom[70] & savory & Onion a little Mace & lemon peel, a little white wine and thicken it up with flour & butter

29

To stew Piggeons brown

Take a piece of fat & lean bacon, & a piece of butter, let this brown in the stew pan, & when you have stuff'd your Piggeon put them into the pan & brown them, when they are brown all over put to it an onion a bundle of sweet herbs put to them warm water enough to cover them, with an anchovy, put the jiblets in it will help the gravy, when it is enough strain it & put to it a piece of butter & a little flour.

30

---

68. Especially thin pieces of meat.
69. A practice to tenderize meat.
70. Marjoram, or *Origanum majorana*, a close relative of oregano but with a sweeter, milder taste and subtle citrus notes.

To make Gooseberry Vinegar

Bruise gooseberries full ripe in a Mortar, then measure them ~~& to every~~ & to every quart of gooseberries put three quarts of water first boil'd, & let it stand to be cold then [put] water to the gooseberries & let it stand 24 hours, then strain it through canvas & then fla[nnel][71] & to every gallon of this liquor put one pound of feeding brown sugar;[72] stir it well together and barrel it up. At three quarters of a year it will be fit for use but if it stands longer it is better. This Vinegar is like-wise good for Pickles.

never Stop down Your Barrel [annotation]

31

To Hash a Calves Head

Boil yr: Calves head 'till the meat is near enough for eating, take it up & cut it in pieces then take half a pint of whitewine, & three quarters of a pint of gravy or strong broth, put [in][73] this liquor two anchovies, half a nutmeg, a little mace, & a small onion stuck with cloves, boil this up in the liquor a quarter of an hour, then strain, it, & let it ~~stand~~ boil up again, when it does so throw in the meat with a little salt to yr: taste, & some lemon peel sliced fine, let it stew a little, & if you please add sweet breads, make force meat balls of veal, mix the brains with the yolk of eggs, & fry them to lay for garnish; when the Head is ready to be sent in, shake in a bit of Butter.

32

---

71. Insertions from Mason, *The Lady's Assistant*, p. 311. The recipe instructs the cook to pass the vinegar through cloths that are successively denser, first canvas and then flannel, to effectively remove all particles of remaining solids.

72. Brown sugar was considerably cheaper than white sugar and sometimes used to fatten livestock, especially pigs.

73. Insertion from Elizabeth Raffald, *The Experienced English Housekeeper*, 1786, p. 85.

To Jugg[74] Beef Steakes with Potatoes

Take rump Steakes, beat them well, pepper & salt them, then take a soup-pot, put at the bottom a little fresh ~~lard~~ butter, a row of Stakes, a row of Potatoes, & so on 'till 'tis full; then fill some gravy or broth, just enough to cover it, let it stew for three hours, then strain it all off & skim all the fat from it; thicken it up with butter & flour, then put it over the steakes again; give it one boil up, & taste if salt enough.

To make almond Cheese-cakes

Take half a p^d: of blanch'd almonds pounded small with a spoonful of Orange flower water & half a pound of double refined sugar 10 yolks of Eggs well beaten add the peels of two oranges or Lemons which must be ~~beaten~~ boil'd very tender then beat in a Mortar very fine then mix them altogether & put in three quarters of a pound of melted butter being almost cold & bake it in good Crust.

33

Lemon Mince Pies

Take a good Lemon, squeese out the Juice; boil the [later annotation: Pulp with the] rind tender, & pound it very fine; put to it three quarters of a pound of currants, half a p^d: of Sugar, half an oz: of Orange flour water a good glass of Mountain[75] or Brandy put ~~to it~~ in your juice with half a Nutmeg a little Mace Cittron or candied Orange peel as you please. You must put three quarters of a p^d: of Beef Suet Chopt very fine & mixed with the Currants. [Later annotation:] Half a doz. Apples chopt fine & added to it, is a great improvement.

---

74. A process whereby meat or game is stewed slowly in a deep pot, usually an earthenware jug, sometimes set in a bath of boiling water.

75. Mountain wine, a sweet wine from the hills around Malaga, Spain, that was popular in the late eighteenth and early nineteenth centuries.

A good Cheese cake with Curd

To a p^d: of & half of Cheese curd put 10 oz: of butter; beat both in
a Mortar till all looks like butter. Then add a quarter of a pound
of Almonds beat fine fine with Orange flower water; 3 quartes of a
pound of Sugar, 8 Eggs, half ye whites; a little Mace pounded, & a
little cream; beat all together a quarter of an hour; bake them in puff
paste[76] & in a quick Oven.

34

Sausages

Take a pound of veal, a pound of Pork, & a pound of Suet; take
the skin & fat from the pork, & Veal, & skin the Suet. Then put it
together & chop it very fine, then put a little Thyme chopt, & some
pepper & salt, & chop it altogether; then mix it up with yolks of Eggs
that it may be stiff.

35

A Trifle

Take three Naple Biscuits[77] cut them in Slices dip them in sack lay
them in the bottom of your dish then make a custard of a pint of
cream & five Eggs & put over them then make a whipt Syllabub[78]
as light as possible to cover the whole the higher it is piled the
handsomer it looks.

---

76. A light and flaky pastry made from compressed layers of dough and butter; now
called puff pastry.

77. A simple, crisp biscuit made from sugar, flour, butter, eggs and rose water.
(Mason, *The Lady's Assistant*, p. 407.) Compares loosely with today's sponge finger.

78. A froth of whipped cream curdled with an acidic liquid (e.g. lemon or orange
juice), sweetened with sugar and flavoured with alcohol (e.g. wine or sherry). (Mason,
The Lady's Assistant, p. 448.)

To make Elder wine

To two Gallons of Water put one Gallon of Berries full ripe & three pounds of Sugar to one Gallon of liquor first boil the Water & the Berries three quarters of an hour, strain the Berries out then boil only half the Sugar in the liquor a quarter of an hour & skim it then put it boiling on the other part of the Sugar in the tub you intend to work it in. Stir it well together let it stand eight & forty hours, then spread a toast with Yeast on both sides well & work it till it has a good head skim off the Barm before you tun it dont stop it down close for a week or more if your Barrel is full.

36

A Two-penny[79] Pudding

Take 2 Spoonfuls of flour weted with cold milk than add near a pint of Boiling with a little grated Lemon peel four Eggs well beat to be put to it when cold with a Spoonful of Powder Sugar[80] Boil it in a dish 3 Quarters of an hour

37

Soup Curry

Take a good Knuckle of Veal, put it up to boil with a Couple of Onions stuck with half a dozen Cloves. let it boil very gently till the Veal is tender. then take it out & cut it from the bone, into large dice. then take two large spoonfuls of rice;[81] parch it before the fire, beat it in a Mortar & put it through a Lawn Sieve,[82] take two

---

79. Or tuppenny. Two pennies, or tuppence, was a low monetary value used to indicate something common or readily available. The description compares with today's recipes categorized as simple or quick and easy.

80. Sugar pounded so finely that the granules are reduced to a powder. Compares with today's icing sugar or confectioner's powdered sugar.

81. Rice prepared as instructed (parched, beaten, sieved) creates rice flour, a thickening agent.

82. Made from a wooden band strung with closely placed material to form a mesh.

ounces of Butter, the flour of Rice & a large Onion choped small, put altogether into your stew pan, & put to them the broth & the Meat which you have cut from the bone. let simmer very gently till the meat is enough. then put into it two tea spoonfuls of Termeric[83] & season it with Chyan & black pepper to your taste. some rice boil'd dry must be serv'd up in a separate dish with it the rice is to be boil'd in a large quantity of water and it must be thrown in when the water is boiling very fast, & with it a handful of salt.

38

A good Sauce for fish, or any Made Dishes

Take a pint of Port wine, twelve anchovies, a quarter of a pint of Vinegar, as much beaten pepper a will as will lay on a Crown piece,[84] two or three Cloves a little Mace, one Nutmeg a small Onion, two Bay leaves, a little Thyme & Parsley & two Bits of Horseradish; put all this in a sauce-pan till all the anchovies are dissolv'd; then strain it off & when cold bottle it. It will keep half a Year in a Cool place. Melt your Butter thick & put in of this Mixture according to your palate.

39

A Baked Apple Pudding

Take a Dozen of Pippins,[85] pulp them through a Cullender, take six eggs, Sugar enough to make Sweet, the rhind of two Lemons grated, a quarter of a pd: of Butter melted without flour or water,[86] Squeeze

---

83. Ground turmeric, a spice of the ginger family with a deep orange-yellow colour.

84. Based on the diameter of a late Georgian crown coin (38 mm or 1½ inch), roughly 1 teaspoon of pepper.

85. Here pippin could refer to an apple seedling or one of a number of apple varieties, such as the Newtown or Albermarle Pippin, grown in southern counties like Hampshire during the mid eighteenth century.

86. A recipe calling for melted butter usually indicated a butter-and-water sauce thickened with flour, hence the need to instruct the cook to simply melt the butter alone.

the juice of two Lemons, let the apples be cold before the ingredients are put together make a puff paste in the bottom of the dish. Half an Hour bakes it.

Jaune Mange

Steep two Oz: of Isinglass an Hour in a pint of Boiling water & if not dissolv'd in that time set it over the fire till it is; then strain it through a clean sive and let it stand a few minutes to settle, Then pour it into a Sauce pan & put near a pint of whitewine & the juice of two Oranges or one Lemon & the peel of one & the Yolks of eight eggs sweeten to your taste with Loaf Sugar,[87] Set it ~~stand~~ over the fire, and keep it stirring till it just boil's up & then strain it off into cups which must be wetted that they may turn out easily.

40

[remainder of manuscript page left blank]

41

To make Soy

Take one hundred of Walnuts, when they are fit to pickle, & pound them small as can be, Add two ~~spoonfuls~~ Handfuls of Salt; the next day put a quart of the best vinegar to them, let them lie open to the Air till they are quite black, stirring them two or three times a day then put a Quart of Strong Beer, & boil it ten minutes, then strain it off & let it stand till the next day then pour off the clear, & to that add a bottle of Port wine, & a head of Garlic cut small, the peel of a Lemon, & a bundle of sweet herbs, half a p^d: of Anchovies; boil all these together a quarter of an hour, then strain it off, then put into it Mace & Jamaca pepper of each half an ounce (whilst 'tis hot) when cold bottle it, 'tis not fit for use under 2 or 3 Months—Its excellent for all brown gravies, it makes fine fish Sauce & will keep 20 Years.

---

87. White or refined sugar was purchased in large cones commonly called loaves. A typical family-sized loaf of sugar weighed between 11 and 13 pounds. The cook used sugar nippers or a sugar hammer to break the loaf into smaller pieces or lumps. For fine granules, the cook pounded the lumps in a mortar with a pestle.

To make little Patties to fry

Take the kidney of a Loin of Veal or Lamb fat & all, shred it very small, season it with a little Salt, Cloves & Nutmeg, all beaten small, some Sugar & ye yoalks of two or three Eggs hard, mince'd very fine, mix all these together with a little sack or Cream, put them into puff paste & fry them.

Thin Cream Pancake, call'd Quire of paper[88]

Take to a pint of cream eight eggs leaving out two whites,[89] three spoonfuls of fine flour 3 spoonfuls of Sack & one spoonful of Orange flower water a little sugar a grated Nutmeg, & a quarter of a p^d: of butter melted in the cream, mingle all well together, mixing the flour with a little cream at first that it may be smooth: butter your pan for the first Pancake, and let them run as thin as possible to be whole; when one side is coulored it is enough, take them carefully out of the pan, & strew some fine sifted sugar between each. lay them as even on each other as you can, this quantity will make twenty

Fish Sauce

Crawfish shels pounded in a stone Mortar put some thin gravy to them, a bit of crust of bread stew this altogether till it is very strong then strain it off & mix it with butter & anchovy.

---

88. According to English typefounder William Caslon, typical quires of paper included either 24 or 25 sheets. Paper was packed between bundles of slightly damaged sheets called 'cording quires', containing 20 sheets – the number of pancakes this recipe yields.
89. Six whole eggs plus two egg yolks.

A very good Orange Pudding

Pare the Yellow rind of two fair Oranges so very thin that no part of the white comes off with it or grate them with a nutmeg grater add to it half a p^d of butter & the Yolks of 16 Eggs beat altogether in a stone mortar 'till it's all of a colour, then pour it into your dish in which you have laid a sheet of puff Paste three quarters of an hour bakes it.

A Bread Pudding

Take half a p^d: of bread, half a p^d: of Suet, half a p^d: of currants, & half a p^d: of Sugar, four eggs, boil it between three & four hours.

Sauce for A Carp

Put into a quarter of a pint of good gravy one Anchovy shred small, a race of ginger bruised, a bit of thyme, a bit of bread crumbled small, let this boil a little while, then put in near a p^d: of butter, some of which must be mix'd with flour to make the sauce thick, & when it has just boil'd as butter does, put in a spoonful of catchup, the blood of the Carp & half a Lemon squeeze'd, take out the thime & ginger. The Carp must be bled in two or three spoonfuls of red wine, in a pewter plate, keept stirring all the time they bleed; they must not be boil'd in much more water than will cover them. You M must put in above half a pint of Vinegar or ~~Vargice~~ Varjuice[90] in the water you boil them in, a bunch of sweet herbs, an Onion a race of ginger some bruised Lemon peel & a piece of Lemon.

---

90. Verjuice, the highly acidic juice of unripe grapes, tart apples or other sour fruit with lemon, herbs or spices added for flavour.

Almond Cream

Blanch & beat half a p^d: of Almonds & boil them in a quart of Cream, then take the Whites of four Eggs well beat sweeten it to your taste with Sugar & With a little Orange flower water add it to the cream & keep it on the fire till ready to boil: keep it stirring all the time.

To Make Ollivers Biscuits[91]

Take a p^d: of flour, half a pint of small beer[92] barm take some Milk & warm it a little put it to your barm & lay a spunge[93] let it lay for one hour then take a quarter of a p^d: of Butter & warm up with some Milk & mix up your spunge & lay it to rise before the fire roll it out in thin Cakes, bake it in a slow oven, you must put a little salt in your flour, but not much rise them before the ~~Oven~~ fire before you but them in the oven.

To Make Ratafia[94] *Cakes*

Take 8 oz: of apricot kernels,[95] if they cannot be had bitter Almonds will do as well, blanch them & beat them very fine with a little Orrange flower water, mix them with the whites of three eggs well beaten & put to them two pounds of single refin'd Sugar finely beaten & sifted, work all together and it will be like a paste, then lay it in little ~~thin plates~~ round bits on tin plates flour'd, set them in an oven that is not very hot & they will puff up & be soon be baked.

---

91. Simple digestive biscuits developed by Dr William Oliver in Bath around 1750.
92. Beer with a low alcohol content. An acceptable beverage for families and servants because several glasses could be consumed without causing intoxication.
93. Usually a piece of bread or toast spread with beer barm, the yeasty scum or foam produced during the brewing process.
94. A sweet, alcoholic beverage similar to brandy, or an essence, with flavouring derived from nuts or fruit kernels.
95. The seed found inside the fruit's stone, now known to be toxic.

Sugar Vinegar

To 12 gallons of water add 14 p^d: of Sugar, put the whole of the sugar into six gallons of the water, boil it and skim it as long as the is any scum rises, then pour it boiling hot into the Vessel & fill it up with the other six Gal. of cold water, when almost cold toast a slice of bread spread it over with Yeast & put it into the Vessel let it work two or three days, then paste a strong brown paper over the bung hole,[96] prick it full of holes, lay a tile over ~~the~~ it then set the cask in the Sun or a warm place till sour, which will be in six weeks or two Months.

48

[remainder of manuscript page left blank]

49

To Pickle Mellons

Make a Strong brine that will bear an Egg[97] then throw it scalding hot on the Mellon. let them lie in it two days then take them out and cut them down the middle take out the inside fill them up with equal quantities of mustard seeds, ginger bruised, & scliced Garlick—then take the best white-wine vinegar and boil in it a Sufficient quantity of Cloves—Mace—pepper and Nutmegs throwgh it on the Mellons scalding hot 3 or 4 Days till they look green—cover them close and keep them for Use—they must be cover'd close every time they are scalded.

    N.B. Cucumbers are done the same way.

---

96. The hole, often plugged by a cork, from which a cask is emptied. The direction to cover the opening with a hole-pricked paper indicates that the vinegar requires aeration.

97. Brine made salty enough for an egg to float in it. 'Make a strong pickle, with cold spring-water and bay-salt, strong enough to bear an egg.' (Glasse, *The Art of Cookery*, p. 150.)

To Pickle Mushroom brown

Take the dirt off the Mushrooms & stalks & the red gills out of them, peel the flaps wash them in Vinegar, then put them into as much Vinegar as will cover them—stew them 'till tender with all sorts of spice exept Cinnamon a little salt, some shalotts & Anchovies—bottle them for Use

The Buttons must be rubb'd with flannel

To preserve Currants

Extract Juice from Currants as you do for Jelly & to every pint of liquor put three quarters of a p^d: of Sugar when boil'd so as to jelly, put into it as many pounds of Currants stript from the stalks as you had pints of liquor let them simmer a short time & then put them into the jars or Glasses.

Fricassee Turnips

Cut your Turnips in dice, when boiled and put a little cream to them Thicken'd with flour & add a little lump Sugar to your taste.

—Mrs. Dundas

A Receipt to Curry after the India Manner

Cut two Chickens as for fricasseeing, wash them clean & put them in a stew pan with as much water as will cover them, with a large spoonful of salt sprinkle them & let them boil till tender covered close all the time, skim them well; when boiled enough take up the Chickens & put the liquor of them in a pan, then put half a pound of fresh butter in the pan & brown it a little, put into it two cloves of garlic & a large onion diced & let these all fry till brown often shaking the pan, then put in Chickens & sprinkle over them two or three spoonfuls of curry powder, then cover them close & let the

Chickens do till brown frequently shaking the Pan, then put in the Liquor the Chickens were boiled in & let all stew till tender. If acid is agreeable squeeze the juice of a Lemon or Orange in to it.

52

A Dish of rice to be boiled, & served up by itself.

Take half a pound of Rice wash it clean in salt and water then put into it two Quarts of boiling water & boil it briskly for twenty minutes then strain it through a Cullender & shake it into a Dish, but do not touch it.

NB—Beef Veal Rabbits Fish &c. may be Curried with or without Rice.

53

To Pickle Pattigonion[98]

Take a full ripe Cucumber, cut it down the middle and take out all the seeds, cut it in square pieces lay them in an earthen pan, cover them over with salt, let them stand 24 hours, then wipe them quite dry, put them in a pot with half a pint of white-Mustard-Seed. 2 oz of long Pepper,[99] 2 oz of shallots, 1 oz of Garlick, 1 oz of Roccombole,[100] a large piece of horse-radish sliced, 6 Bay leaves, half a dz cloves, 3 or 4 blades of Mace,[101] & a little Ginger. Then boil Vinegar enough to cover them & pour on them, cover them close & let them stand 24 hours, then boil the Vinegar as before do so 3 or 4 times the last time put all your pieces in let them boil up 5 minutes & then put them into your Pickle pot cover it up till the next day, then tye them close for use.

---

98. Patagonian cucumbers, a long and slender variety named after its region of origin at the southern tip of South America.
99. The dried immature fruits of the flowering vine *Piper longum* or *Piper retrofractum*, with a taste similar to but hotter than black peppercorns.
100. Rocambole or *Allium scorodoprasum*, a European sand leek of the amaryllis family. The bulbous plant has a pungent odour similar to onion and is used as a seasoning.
101. Sections of the outer membrane surrounding a nutmeg seed. When dried, the membrane is pounded to form powdered mace.

India Pickel

Take white Cabbage or Cauliflower, cut them in quarters, & boil
them one minute, put a little salt in the water then seperate them leaf
from leaf on a tin to dry them, put them into the following pickel.
One gallon of Vinegar one oz: of long pepper a q^r: p^d: of Ginger,
an oz: of Jamaica pepper half a pint of Mustard seed bruised, an oz:
of Termeric & a p^d: of garlick boiled salted & dried as the cabbage,
cover your pickel boiling & let it stand to be cold before you put in
the cabbage. Any thing else may be done in the same manner

To Candy angelica[102]

When your Angelica is young cut it in lengths boil it in salt & water
till it is tender & green dry it in clothes, & to every p^d: of ~~Sugar~~ stalks
put one p^d: of fine Sugar, lay your stalks in an earthen pan, pound y^e
Sugar & strew it over them, then let them stand two days, after which
boil them till they are ~~tender~~ clear & strain them from your Syrup,
beat another p^d: of sugar very fine, & strew it on your Angelica
lay it on plates to dry & put~~h~~ it into your Oven after the pies are
drawn, turning them frequently on clean plates ~~had~~. NB If you find it
difficult to preserve them green, when it is boiling make use of Vine
leaves.[103]

---

102. *Angelica archangelica*, a sweetly scented herb with lacy white flowers and hollow
stems, known commonly as wild celery. Both the stems and flowers are edible and
often prepared as candy and cake decorations.

103. This note was probably written at some earlier point by an individual cook.
It was not printed in the most common period sources, but appears in the original
hand in this entry and its duplicate on manuscript p. 57. According to contemporary
sources, the only leaves used for green food colouring were spinach, which is a
plant rather than a vine. For angelica, 'if it be a good green, boil it no more; if not,
heat it again, and the day following boil the sugar till it is very smooth, and pour it
upon your angelica.' (Hannah Glasse, *The Complete Confectioner*, 1800, p. 14.) Other
publications have similar instructions.

Resoles[104]

Take a p^d of Veal (which has been roasted) a little Suet, a qr^r: of a p^d: of butter & a little lemon peel, chop all these together very fine & then beat them in a Mortar, add a little lemon pickel to your taste & a little very good cream fry your resoles in Mutton suet what shape you like best. NB Minced Veal is very good done in the same way mixed as above.

56

Lemon Pickles

One Doz: of Lemon ~~pickel~~ the out rind peel grated very fine off, cut them into four quarters leaving the bottom <u>whole</u>, then rub upon them equally ½ a p^d of Bay salt, & spread them upon a large <u>pewter</u> dish, set them into the sun to dry gradually until all the juice is dried into the peel, after which put your lemons into a pitcher with an oz: of mace, half an oz: of cloves beat fine, 1 oz: of Nutmegs cut into thin pieces, four oz: of Garlic pulled, & half a pint of Mustard seed bruised a little, tie all these together in a Muslin bag & pour two quarts of white wine vinegar upon them. Close your pitcher well up, & let it stand for five or six days by the fire shaking it up sometimes then tie it up for three months To take off the bitterness, when you bottle it put your lemons & liquor into a hair sive press them to get out the liquor & let it stand another day then pour off the fine & bottle it let the other stand a day or two till it has refined itself so till the whole is bottled.

N.B. You may add ~~your~~ one quart of ~~or~~ Vinegar to the ingredients & let it stand a month or two & it will be equally good. This pickle is much better for being a longer time upon the lemons than the receipt say's, & will keep for years

---

104. Rissoles: fried patties of minced meat and savoury flavourings. Today's rissoles often incorporate breadcrumbs either with the meat or as a coating for a crisp outer crust.

To candy Angelica

When your Angelica is young & ~~tender~~ cut it in lengths, boil it in salt & water till it is quite tender & green, dry it in clothes, & to every p^d: of stalks put one p^d: of fine sugar, lay y^r stalks in an earthen pan pound the sugar & strew over them, then let them stand two days, after which boil them 'till they are clear & strain them from y^r Syrup, beat another p^d: of Sugar very fine & strew over your Angelica lay it on plates to dry, & put them into your oven after your pies are drawn turning them constantly on clean plates.—NB If you find it difficult to preserve them green, when it is boiling, use Vine leaves

Mrs. Davisons receipt to pickle Pork or Beef [105]

To four Gallons of water put a p^d: ½ of coarse sugar two oz: of salt petre, & six p^ds: of Bay salt into a large pan & let it boil, being careful to take off the scum as it rises, when no more scum rises take ye pan off ye fire & let it stand to cool then put your meat into the vessel where it is to remain & pour ye pickle over it till all is cover'd. NB. Beef & Mutton will roast after lying in the pickle a day or two, & pork is excellent. Remember to wash the meat well before you use it.

To dress a Breast of Mutton

Boil your Breast of Mutton 'till the bones will slip out, take off the skin & rub the meat over with yolk of egg, A few sweet herbs, parsley, Onion, & crumbs of bread, with pepper & salt choped altogether & strewed over the meat, put it in a dutch oven [106] before a fire to brown, dish it up with a rich gravy.

---

105. Unlike other instructions to pickle meat for preservation, this recipe uses pickling liquid to marinate meat for roasting. The salty pickle helps the meat retain moisture during cooking, just as brining meat does today.

106. The term 'Dutch oven' refers to two different cooking tools: (1) A semi-circular sheet of reflective metal placed hearthside behind food to brown it. This was also

India Pickles

Take half a p^d: of Ginger put it in water one night scrape it & cut
it in thin slices put it in a bowl with dry salt & let it stand till your
other ingredients are fit. Take half a p^d: of Garlic, peel & cut it in
pieces put it in dry salt three days then wash it and put it in the sun
to dry. Take a q^r: of a p^d: of Mustard seed bruised very fine; an oz:
of Termrick, a Gallon of the strongest vinegar, put these ingredients
into a stone jar, let it be three parts full. Take white Cabbage, &
quarter it keep it in dry salt three days then dry it into the Sun. So
do Calliflowers Cucumbers, Mellons, Peaches, plums Apples or any
thing you of this sort. Radishes may be done the same way leaving
on the young tops, also french beans & asparagus the three last are
to be salted but two days & dried as the others. You need not empty
your jar, but as things come in season put them in and fill it up with
fresh vinegar. The more every thing is dried in the sun the plumper
it will be in the pickle, if the pickles are not high colour'd enough,
add a little more term'ric which makes it the colour of the india
Mango. Never put red Cabbage or Walnuts because because they
spoil & discoulor all the rest

Biscuits

—M^rs. Dundas

Take two oz: of lard or butter, & two lb of of flour, mix them well
together stiff with a little cold water, work or knead them very well roll
your biscuits very thin, & prick them exceedingly, bake them on tins in
a very quick Oven, looking constantly at them or they will scorch.

---

called a reflecting oven, reflecting pan or hastener. At some point, the sheet was fitted
with a spit for roasting joints of meat, similar to today's rotisserie. (2) A cooking pot
with thick sides and a tight-fitting lid, most commonly of cast iron. Hot coals from the
fire were placed on the pot's flat lid to raise the temperature and cook the food within.
The recipe probably refers to a Dutch oven of the first description.

Orange or Lemon Juice

To three p^d: of Sugar (fine lump) but one quart of juice let it stand ten days, then take the scum quite clear off, Run it through a jelly bag & bottle it for use—do not cork your bottles, but put a piece of paper over the mouth.

61

Bolton Bunns[107]

Rub a quarter of a p^d: of Butter into 2 p^d: of flour, a q^r: of a p^d: of Sugar, a handful of Currants, two spoonfuls of good yeast, set it to rise before the fire the yolks of two Eggs and about a pint of warm milk, wet it into a limp paste; & make it into forty Bunns.

An excellent Fish Sause

—M^rs. Fowle

Take a pint of Port wine, 12 anchovies, a quarter ~~Salt~~ of a pint of Vinegar, as much beaten pepper as will lay on a half crown, two or three cloves, a little Mace, one Nutmeg, a small Onion, two bay leaves a little Thyme & parsley, two bits of radish put all this into a sause pan and let it simmer 'till all the Anchovies are disolved then strain it off & when cold bottle it for use—It will keep 12 Months in a cool place—Melt your butter thick & put in of this mixture to your palate.

---

107. Possibly named for the town of Bolton, near Manchester, with a history of cottage spinning and weaving. Notable improvements in spinning technology were made in Bolton shortly after Martha began collecting recipes.

Mock Turtle

—Mʳˢ. Fowle

Take a large calves head scald ~~th~~ off the hair, boil it 'till the horn
is tender, then cut it into slices about the size of your finger, with as
little lean as possible: have ready near three pints of good mutton or
Veal ~~gravy~~ broth, put to it half a pint of Meaderia Wine, half a tea
spoonful of Chyan pepper, a large Onion, & the peel of a Lemon
chopt very small, a quarter of a pint of Oysters chopt, & their liquor,
a little salt, the juice of two large lemons, some sweet herbs, & the
brains chopt, stew all these together about an hour, & send it to table
with forced meat balls made small, & the Yolks of hard Eggs.

63

To dry Mushrooms

Take a peck of Mushrooms without taking out the combs, peel
the biggest & wash the others, then put them into a kettle with 12
Onions, two handfuls of Salt, a good quantity of pepper, cloves,
mace, nutmegs, & some bay leaves, then hang them on the fire, & let
them boil 'till almost all the liquor is consumed, often stirring them
about, & when they can boil no longer for fear of burning, stir into
them about half a pᵈ: of butter, & when they are cold pick them out
& lay them single on earthen platters, & set them into the oven as
soon as you have drawn your bread, & so do as often as you bake
'till they are throughly dry, then beat them into a powder, & put it
up close in a gallipot:[108] a Spoonful of this ~~liquor~~ powder gives a rich
taste to any made dish, & helps to thicken the sauce.

64

[manuscript page left blank]

---

108. A small glazed pot used to store medicines.

Potatoe Yeast

Poil Potatoes of the mealy kind till they are quite soft, skin, & mash them, add as much hot water as will make them the consistency of yeast but not thicker. To every p^d: of Potatoes put two oz: of course sugar or treacle & when just warm to every p^d: of Potatoes put two spoonfuls of yeast keep it warm till it has done fermenting, & in 24 hours it may be used, A p^d: of Potatoes will make a quart of yeast. when made it will keep three months, lay the bread eight hours before you ~~make~~ bake it.

NB For present use it will do very well if your potatoes are put to the Yeast the night before, or even two or three hours.

Fish Sauce

Two Anchovies Simmer'd in a little Water 'till dissolved & a little horseradish to be boiled with it two spoonfuls of Elder Vinegar three or four spoonfuls of White Wine, A little Mushroom catchup and to be thickend with Butter & flour.

A Harrico of Mutton[109]

Cut a Neck of Mutton into ~~Stake~~ Steaks flour them & fry them Brown on each side. put into your stew pan a piece of Butter & two spoonfuls of flour, & let is simmer together 'till it is of a light brown keeping it stirring all the time add to it some good Gravy & let it boil up, Then put in your steaks, & Turnips & Carrots, & let it stew one hour pepper & Salt it to your taste & two spoonfuls of Catchup. When done, if Greasy mix some flour with cold water and put in to it, but let it only boil up once afterwards.

---

109. Based on the classic French dish *haricot de mouton*, lamb stewed in a highly seasoned sauce. The dish does not contain haricot beans, as its name might suggest, but derives from the Old French *harigoter*, to cut up.

Rasberry Vinegar[110]

Put two quarts of large fine Rasberries into one quart of the best Vin'gar, let it stand 10 days near a fire, clarify 2 p^ds: of fine Sugar, strain off the juice from the Rasberries, add the clarified Syrup & boil all together 'till it is fine. When it is cold put it into small Bottles & use it as you would Orgeat,[111] mix it with Water to your taste.— M^rs. Lefroy

Orange Jelly

An oz: of Isinglass boiled in a pint of Water, add to it the juice of four China Oranges[112] & one Lemon, & one Seville Orange, boil it again with a little of the Lemon Peel, & some Lump Sugar—Strain it through any thing thin.[113]

Snow Cheese

Take one ~~to~~ a pint of cream grate the Peel of two Lemons, & squeeze the juice of them into it with sugar to your taste, whisk it up to a consistency put it into a small Lawn sive & let it ~~stand up~~ drain twenty four hours & then turn it into your dish & serve it up with sweetmeats or what you like.

---

110. Martha collected recipes for two types of Raspberry Vinegar: one served by the glass as a beverage, the other dosed by the teaspoon as a medicine.

111. A refreshing drink originally made from pounded sweet and bitter almonds, the juice and peel of oranges and lemons, sugar and water. (Mason, *The Lady's Assistant*, p. 454.) Bitter almonds are now known to be toxic.

112. A general term for sweet oranges, named after the country where the hybrid was first developed. In this recipe, sweet China oranges balance the tartness of Seville oranges.

113. Any thin, closely woven cloth bag used to strain the solids from the liquid.

Pink Vinegar

Two quarts of the best whitewine Vinegar one pint of Port wine, four table spoonfuls of Anchovyes liquor two table spoonfuls of Walnut Catchup 30 or 40 shallots two table spoonfuls of India Soy, 1 oz: of Chyan pepper 1 oz: of Cocheneal,[114] add two Horse-radish, Lemon pickel peel & spice to your taste. Boil it a quarter of an hour & strain it off, let it stand till the next day then Bottle it.

69

To keep Mushrooms as fresh gather'd

Take midle sized Mushrooms that are pretty close rub them with flannel & throw them into milk & water; & salt change your water after they have lain some a little time: then wash them well, put them into a sause pan with a very little water then th___ strew some salt over them, a little whole pepper, mace and an Onion, let them boil a quarter of an hour very quick, then put them into a cullender when they are drained spread them on a coarse Cloth, & cover them close 'till they are cold having first prepared brine as strong as will bear an egg with an Onion, & some whole pepper boild in it. When it is cold, & the mushrooms also, put as many of them into a wide mouthed bottle as it will hold, then fill the bottle up with brine taking the Onion out cork the bottle as close as fow possible & set them in a Cellar with the corks downwards. When you would use them lay them in scalding water, & Milk, change the water, & milk several times 'till you think them fresh enough either to fricasee or to put into any made dish.

70

114. Cochineal, a red dye derived from dried female insects of the same name, used primarily in beverages and cosmetics.

To pickle Mushrooms brown

Take the dirt off the Mushrooms and the Gills; & stalks from out
of them peel the flaps wash them in Vinegar, then put them into as
much vinegar as will cover them stew them 'till tender with all sorts
of spices except Cinnamon a little salt some shallots, & Anchovies,
bottle them for use

   N:B: The buttons to be rubbed with flannel—it is better to pour
the vinegar boiling on the spices instead of stewing them with the
mushrooms.

71

To make an Orange Pudding

Take the yolks of 12 eggs well beaten 1 p^d: of loaf sugar pounded,
three oz: of candied Orange peel sliced, three quarters of a p^d: of
fresh butter clarified—Mix all these together, & bake them in a dish
with puff paste under & over it, the oven being moderately hot—it
will bake it in less than an hour.

To make Cow heel Soup

Make a strong gravy with a shin of Beef a p^r. of Cow heels boild
tender, then cut them in pieces & take out the large bones, one hour
before dinner, season the gravy with knotted Marjoram, savory
Thyme, the green of Onions, parsley, & shalots, chopt fine of each a
Tea spoonful half a pint of Madeira or Sherry, four large spoonfuls of
Walnut, & two of Mushroom Catchup, pepper, & salt to your taste—
flour the feet, & put them in a stew pan with the gravy, & just before
it is sent to table take a little of the soup almost cold, the Yolks of two
eggs, & a little flour beat well together in a sauce pan then boil it up
& put it to the soup & then give it all one boil up.

72

Vegetable Pie

Take as many vegetables as are in season, Cabbage, Turnips, Carrots, Cucumbers, & Onion, fry them in Butter, when well fry'd drain, & season them with pepper & salt & lay them in layers in your dish on crust cover them with a crust, have ready some good gravy to put into the pie when baked. It must not be put into a very hot oven.

To pickel Lemons

Take Six Lemons of the largest size, grate them all over slightly, cut across the knob end and rub in some salt very thoroughly, lay them in a jar well cover'd with salt, in a warm place for near a fortnight, then take them from the salt, & quite cover them with raw Vinegar, take a bit of thin cloth the size of the top of the jar, & put into it a pint of white Mustard seed, some sliced ginger, & horse radish—they will not be fit for use under two months, & the longer they are kept the better they are.

73

Receipt to make Lemon Pickles

—Lady Williams

Take Six large Lemons or a Doz: small ones have them thick cut them into eight half quarters. One pound of Salt, six large Cloves of Garlic, two oz: of horse radish sliced thin two quarts of the best Vinegar Nutmegs, Mace Cloves, & Cayenne pepper, of each a quarter of an oz:, two oz: of the best flower of Mustard:[115]—let it boil a ~~th~~ quarter of an hour, then set it by & stir it once or twice a day for a fortnight, then strain it off, & bottle it for use.

---

115. Mustard flour: the seeds of the mustard plant, ground to make a yellow powder.

Very good white Sauce for boil'd Carp

Take half a p^d: of Veal, cut it into small pieces, boil it in a pint of
Water with an Onion, a blade of Mace two Cloves, a few whole
pepper corns, a little salt & Nutmeg, and a bundle of sweet herbs,
'till it is as rich as you would have it.—Strain it off, & put it into your
sauce pan, add to it a piece of butter as big as an egg worked up with
flour, a tea cup full of Cream, a Tea Cup of white Wine, & half a tea
cup of Elder Vinegar. —M^rs. Austen

75

To make Calves feet Jelly

—Miss Lawrence

A set (Two are sufficient if not very small) of Calves feet nicely
cleaned, the skin not taken off; chop the bones, & boil them slowly in
two quarts of water 'till it comes to one.[116] The jelly must stand till the
next day when the fat must be all taken off. Melt the jelly, & put into
it the juice of three lemons, & the peeling cut very thin, three ounces
of loaf sugar a pint of Mountain Wine, & the whites of six eggs beat
into a froth. Let it just boil, & strain it through a Flannel bag.

Garlic Vinegar

A pint of Garlic picked & clean'd—put it into a pint of warm Vinegar
to stand three days—then strain it off and bottle it for use.

—M^rs. Wroughton

To preserve fruit of any kind

Gather the fruit in a dry day—allow a q^r: of a p^d: of brown Sugar
to a p^d: of fruit—put a layer of Sugar at the bottom of the jar then

---

116. Meaning to boil in two quarts of water until the liquid reduces to one quart.

a layer of fruit, & so on till the jar is filled—Tie a Bladder[117] over the mouth of the jar very tight, put it in a bath heated till the Bladder is tight and rises up in the middle take the jar out & let it stand 'till cold, & then tie paper over the bladder—The sweetmeats will not keep long after the bladder is open'd—it is therefore best to do it in small jars.

Barbaries, & Rasberries require a very little more Sugar than other fruit

Pudding

Of Bread, Suet, Apples, Currants, 6 oz: each—5 oz: of Sugar 6 Eggs a little Ratifia—boil it three hours in a Cup.

—Miss Susan Debary

To make Curree Powder[118]

Take of Termeric Root, or Galangal Root[119] each half an oz: Best Cayenne Pepper a quarter of an oz: Let the Termeric or Galangal be reduced to a fine powder separately, then mix them with the other articles & keep for use. NB. Two oz: of Rice powderd to be mixed also with the other ingredients.

—M^{rs}. Jane Fowle

White Soup

Make your gravy of any kind of Meat, add to it the yolks of four Eggs boiled hard & pounded very fine, 2 oz of sweet Almond pounded, as much Cream as will make it of a good Color

---

117. Most likely a section of sheep's bladder.
118. Curry powder.
119. A culinary rhizome of the ginger family, with a similarly hot, spicy flavour.

To make Fish Sauce.

—Cap^{tn}: Austen

Take two Heads of Garlick, cutting each clove in halves; add 1 oz: of Cayenne Pepper, 2 spoonfuls of Indian Soy, 2 oz: of walnut Ketchup or pickle, put them in a Quart Bottle, fill it with cold Vinegar; Cork it close & shake it well—It is fit for use in a Month & will keep good for years.

78

Swiss Soup Meagre

Take four Cabbage Lettuces, 1 Endive, Sorrel Spinnage Cherville, Chives, Onions, Parsley, Beet leaves, Cucumbers sliced, Peas, or Asparaguss; let all these herbs be cut fine & no stalks put in, then put a quarter of a p^d: of Butter in a stew pan, shake over your herbs when they are in the Butter a small spoonful of flour & let them stew some time then pour in a quart of boiling Water & let it stew on till near dinner time; then add the yolks of three Eggs in a tea Cup of Cream, & a Roll if you like it. Broth is better than so much water if you have it. If you have not all the vegetables above mention'd, it will be very good with what you have or a little Seville Orange juice if you like.

79

To Make Orange Wine

Take ten Gal: of Water, 30 lbs of fine Lisbon Sugar & the Whites of 6 Eggs well beaten, boil it together three quarters of an hour skimming it well & then add the juice of 33 Seville Oranges (reserving the Peel of 24 of them to throw into the Barrel) the juice of 36 sweet Oranges & of fifteen Lemons mix all well together & boil it up again—When cold for working take a large toast cover it with good yeast & let it stand work for two days & two nights, then tun it—. Rack it off[120] at

---

120. Racking is an essential step in winemaking, when the liquor is drawn off from the lees or dregs in the barrel.

the end of four months, rinse the Cask & replace the Liquor[121] with
a Bottle of Brandy & three p^d: of Lump Sugar.—You may Bottle it
towards the end of the year.   —Mrs C. Fowle

80

Green Gooseberry Wine

To every pound of Gooseberries (gather'd when green) picked that
is topped & tailed & bruised put one Quart of Water, let it stand
three days stirring it twice every day—To every gallon of juice when
strained put three p^ds: of loaf sugar—Put it into a Barrel & add to
every 20 quarts of liquor one quart of Brandy or a little Isinglass—
Let it stand half a year & then bottle it.   —Miss Thornhill

To make Cheese Puddings

Of Cheshire or Gloucester Cheese take one p^d: and quarter, pound it
in a Mortar with the yolks of three Eggs & the whites of one till it is
a paste—lay it on a Butter'd toast & brown it with a Salamander.[122]
                                                              —M^rs. Dundas

81

To make Hogs Puddings[123]

To half a Gallon of whole Oatmeal well picked and boiled very
tender in milk & water the day before you make your puddings put
the following ingredients: eight Eggs leaving out half the whites, the
rind of a large lemon grated; Penny-royal[124] & leaks chopped very fine

---

121. Meaning either to return the liquor to the cask or to supplement the liquor lost
through evaporation, commonly known as the angels' share.

122. A long rod with a flat iron plate at one end that is thrust into the fire until red
hot then suspended over food. Used here to melt the cheese and brown it lightly.

123. Here pudding refers to sausage, as in black pudding, a traditional sausage
made largely of pork blood.

124. Pennyroyal, an aromatic herb of the mint family with a history of culinary and
medicinal use, now considered toxic.

of each a large spoonful; two teaspoonfuls of Jamaica pepper, & three of common black pepper after it is pounded; half a p^d: of Crumb of bread grated fine; salt to your taste. It must be mixed well together, & cold milk added to it to make it about the consistency of a rice pudding: strain the blood into it 'til it is of as dark a colour as you like, & you must put in a considerable quantity of the fat from the Pig which must be previously cut into pieces the size of a larg nutmeg. When filled and tied up, put them into a Bucket of water to wash them clean from whence they should be taken one by one and put into a kettle of boiling water, make it boil up, and they must continue to do so for an hour; you must be careful to prick them as they rise in the water, or they will burst—take them out carefully with a nice stick & lay them upon clean straw. The puddings are equally good without the Blood, but they will be white instead of black.

82

To cure Bacon

Rub the Flitches[125] over with Salt Petre, particularly observing to force some in where the Hocks[126] are taken off, then take one p^d: of coarse feeding Sugar[127] & as much common salt mixed well together strew it regularly over the flitches cover it over with common salt & press it down close with the hand, let it lay twenty four hours then rub it well & add a little fresh salt, let it be rubbed & changed every other day for a month & then hung up in a chimney where a moderate wood fire is kept for three weeks, and it should afterwards be kept in a Chest with dry straw.

---

125. A flitch is one side of a butchered pig that has been split in half.
126. Also known as pork knuckles, the joint of a butchered pig between the leg and the foot.
127. Inexpensive brown sugar, sometimes used to fatten livestock, especially pigs.

The Salt Petre should be pounded very fine & dryed by the fire—
One p^d: will be sufficient for a Pig weighing eleven Score[128] reserving
enough out of it to rub over the Chines.[129]   —M^rs. Craven

To Pickel Pork

Bone it & cut it in such pieces as will lie most conveniently in a
powdering Tub[130] which must be large & sound[131] to hold Brine, the
narrower & deeper the better it will keep the meat, rub every piece
with salt Petre & then take common salt, rub it over & cover it with
Salt—Strew salt at the bottom of the Tub, lay the pieces in as close
as possible strewing salt round the sides of the Tub; as the salt melts
at the top put on more—The Meat should be pressed with a broad
& heavy stone to keep it under the Brine.—It will keep two years, or
may be used in two Months.

—M^rs. Craven

Ginger Beer

Two Gallons of Water, two oz: of Cream of Tartar[132] Two pounds
of Lump Sugar, Two Lemons sliced, Two oz: of Ginger bruised.—
Pour the water boiling on the ingredients, then add two spoonsful
of good yeast: when cold bottle it in stone Bottles & tie down the
corkes, it is fit to drink in 48 hours.—A little more sugar is an

---

128. A pound of saltpetre used in the recipe will cure a pig weighing 'eleven score'
(i.e. 220 pounds).

129. Pork shins or shanks, a meatier section than the hock.

130. A large container, commonly of wood or stone, in which large sections of meat
are cured with salt. Also known as a salting tub or a powdering trough.

131. i.e. watertight.

132. Potassium bitartrate, the crystals that form as grapes ferment in the wine-
making process. When used in home brewing, cream of tartar helps break up and
stabilize sugar.

improvement; the Corkes are <u>not</u> usually tied down, which saves trouble, & glass Bottles will do.

[manuscript page left blank]

To make a Veal Soup

—M^r. Hartley

Take a Knuckle of Veal and a piece of Ham, put it over the fire with as much Water as will cover it, add three or four Onions, a head of Cellary & sweet herbs; when it boils skim it well—stew it four hours, then take up the meat from the bone & all the Gristle—Take off the fat, strain it through a sieve, thicken it with a little flour & white bread add a little Cream, rub it through a Sieve—then stir it over the fire, & let it have a good boil up—put in your meat & gristle.

To make Gravy or Glaze

Do[133]———

Take a fore Shin of Beef cut it in pieces, & lay it in a stew pan with six large onions—Turnip Carrot, & two heads of Cellary & sweet herbs—set it on a stove & draw out the Gravy, let it be brown & all dried up, then put water to it, skim it very well & let it boil till very good Gravy—then strain it through a sieve, & when it is cold take off all the fat, & take any quantity you want, set it on the side of the Stove without a Cover, & let it boil till it is like glue[134]—put it on any thing you wish to Glaze with a paste brush.

---

133. i.e. another recipe contributed by Mr Hartley.
134. The paste-like consistency enables the gravy or glaze to cling to the meat being cooked.

Fish Sauce

—M^r. Hartley

Eighteen spoonsful of Raisin Wine, 9 do of Vinegar[135] 3 of Walnut
Catchup or Walnut pickle, some Mace a few Cloves & one Nutmeg
cut into three pieces—three large onions & six Anchovies—Let all
these simmer together over a slow fire an hour, then strain it through
a hair Sieve & bottle it for use.

  N.B: How to use the above—
Take half a p^d: of Butter cut it into three slices, flour them & put
them into a sauce pan with six spoonsful of the liquor, set it on the
fire to melt, be careful it does not oil[136]—when quite melted add four
spoonful of Cream & the yolks of two eggs, stir it & pour it into the
boat[137]—If it remain on the fire it will curdle—A little elder Vinegar is
an improvement.

Bread Sauce

—Do

Put some bread Crums into a pan with a small Onion & a little
Gravy, let it boil & then add a little Cream—take out the Onion
before you put it into the boat & add a little salt to your taste

Veal Cake

—Mrs. Dundas

Bone a fat breast of Veal, cut some slices of Ham, the yolks of six
Eggs boiled hard & a handful of parsley chopped fine; cut your Veal
into three pieces, put the fat piece at the bottom of a Cake Tin, then

---

135. 9 spoonfuls of vinegar.
136. Overheating this butter-based sauce causes the mixture to oil, or to separate.
137. Sauce or gravy boat, for serving at the dining table.

season it with pepper salt & the parsley Eggs ~~Mace~~ Ham between each layer, put the thinnest piece of Veal at the Top, & a Coffee cup of Water over it Bake it three Hours in a quick Oven with the bones over it—when done take them off & lay a weight on your meat in a small plate—as it cools the weight must be heavier that the Cake may be close & firm—the Brisket of the Veal is the only part used.

88

Gooseberry Cheese[138]

Take some green goosberrys, put them in a jar, set it in boiling water, till they are soft, then rub them through a sieve, & to every pound of pulp add a pound of sugar—Let it boil ten minutes, if it boil longer it will spoil the colour.   —Mrs. Craven

good luck to your jamming [annotation]

Toasted Cheese

Grate the Cheese & add to it one egg, & a teaspoonful of Mustard, & a little Butter send it up on a toast or in paper Trays.[139]

89

Dryed Gooseberries

—Miss Sharpe

Take six lbs of ripe Gooseberries; put them into a preserving Pan[140] with two lbs of Loaf Sugar powdered & strewed amongst them—Let them simmer until they begin to shrivel then strain them from the juice, lay them on Dishes & dry them upon a hot hearth, or in a

---

138. A jam so thick that it can be cut like cheese, similar to the Spanish *membrillo* or quince cheese, sometimes called quince paste in eighteenth-century cookbooks.
139. The casual presentation of this dish indicates that it is more appropriate for supper than for dinner, the main meal of the day.
140. A large pan with shallow sides, ideal for boiling jams and marmalades. The wide cooking surface enables heat to reach a large portion of the contents while the low sides enable moisture to escape the mixture easily.

cool Oven, taking care not to burn them. The same Syrup will do
another Six pounds.

Noyeau[141]

One ounce of the finest Apricot Kernels, one pound of Sugar
Candy,[142] a <u>small</u> quantity of Cinnamon and Coriander Seed
powdered—Infuse them in a quart Bottle of the best Brandy ~~and a
pint of water~~—Keep it well corked for three weeks, shaking it every
day—After standing a few days to settle run it through a Jelly Bag.

90

Cherry Brandy as a Liquour

Put the Cherries into a Jar & set it in hot Water to draw out the juice
(as you would for Currant Jelly) press it through a Sieve, & to every
Pint of this juice, put three quarters of a pound of very fine Lump
Sugar, boil it & skim it until it is fine, when cold add a pint of Brandy
to every pint of juice—The Stones must be broken & the Kernels put
into the Bottles.

    N.B. Bitter Almonds, or Apricot Kernels are good in it.

—M^{rs}. Craven

    If Morella Cherries[143] are <u>very</u> fine they produce nearly half a pint
of juice to a pound

Solid Custard

In a quart of Milk boil an oz: of Isinglass until the latter is dissolved,
then strain it through a Sive, let it stand a short time add the Yolks
of five Eggs well beaten mix them with the Milk & set it on the fire

---

141. *Crème de noyau*, a French brandy-based liquor flavoured by fruit kernels
(apricots, peaches, plums) and having a taste similar to bitter almonds. These fruit
kernels and bitter almonds are now known to be toxic.
142. Drops or sticks of sugar candy, sometimes made with fruit or other flavourings.
143. Morello cherries are characterized by mahogany-red skin and sour, tart flesh.

until it is as thick as a rich ~~Cream~~ boiled Custard, sweeten & put it into a Mould to prepare it for the Table—A few Bitter Almonds, or a Bay leaf will improve the flavor very much.   —Mrs. Sawbridge

91

To cure Bacon

This receipt used at Portsdown Lodge [annotation]   —Mrs. Fowle
To a Pig weighing fourteen Score—Rub the flitches well over with one pound of Salt Petre finely powdered particularly observing to force some into where the hocks are taken off.—Take one pound of coarse feeding Sugar & as much common Salt mixed well together; strew it regularly over the Flitches, cover it over with common salt, pressing it close down with the hand. Let it lay for five or six days observing as the salt melts to cover it with fresh. Then rub it well & change the flitches every week for six weeks, keeping them still covered with salt.—Hang it up in a Chimney where there is a moderate wood fire kept for three weeks. It should afterwards be kept free from damp.

   N.B. It is found best to put the greatest part of the Sugar & Salt upon the Gammons.[144]

92

To make Noyeau

Two Quarts of common Gin, one pound of Bitter Almonds blanched—Let these ingredients stand in a Stone Jar closely corked until the bitterness be quite extracted then add one pound & half of white Sugar Candy; filter the whole together through blotting paper—If not sufficiently clear, add a little Isinglass—N:B: The Almonds do very well for Puddings afterwards.

—Mrs. Hry. Austen

---

144. Hind legs.

Scotch Orange Marmalade

—Miss Debary

Each lb of Oranges requires 1 lb & ¼ of Lump Sugar. Quarter the
Oranges, then take off the rind & cut part of the white substance
from it—Put the rinds into boiling water & boil them quickly for an
hour & a half or two hours—Slice them as thin as possible—Squeeze
the pulp thro' a sieve, adding a little water to the dregs—Break the
Sugar fine put it in the pan, pour the pulp on it—When dissolved
add the rinds, then boil the whole for twenty minutes—A little
Essence of Lemon may be added before it is taken off the fire in the
proportion of a small tea spoonful to twelve Oranges.

93

Brised Crust[145]

—Mrs. Austen

Two lb of Flour ¼ lb Butter ¼ Lard—Rub the Butter & Lard into a
little milk on the fire as soon as it begins to melt, rub it into the flour,
wet it with some of the hot milk—Make the paste very stiff & keep it
warm whilst you work it up.

Short Crust

—Mrs. Hulbert

A lb of Flour a qr. of a lb of white sugar a qr. of a lb of Butter rubbed
in—To be wetted with three eggs, leaving out one of the whites to
wash the pies on the tops, shaking white sugar over them at the last.

Short Crust

—Mrs. Austen

A pd. of Flour a quarter of a pd. of Butter a qr. of a pd. of Lard
rubbed in & wetted of a moderate stiffness with hot water.

---

145. Anglicized version of the French *pâte brisée*—shortcrust or piecrust pastry.

Macaroni

Stew a quarter of a p^d. of the pipe Macaroni[146] in milk & water until
it is tender, then lay it upon the top of a sive to drain.—Put it into
a stew pan with two large spoonsful of grated parmesan Cheese, a
quarter of a pint of Cream, a small piece of Butter & some salt—
Stew it gently 'till the whole seems well done, then put it into a dish,
strew grated Parmesan Cheese over it, & brown it with a Salamander
or in a Dutch Oven—It may be done with gravy instead of Cream if
prefered.

Mock Oyster Sauce

Take half a pint of Cream, one blade of Mace pounded & boiled
with the Cream, thicken it with butter rolled in flour, & add essence
of Anchovies to your taste; about one spoonful.

To prepare Rice for sweet dishes

Take a q^r. of a pound of the best Carolina Rice[147] & wash it in several
waters, rubbing the rice between the hands 'till the water leaves the
Rice quite clear; then pick it clean & give it one boil in water, strain
it on a sivee, & when free from water put it in a stew pan that will
hold three points, add to it a point of milk, a small piece of cinamon
& Lemon peel. When it has boiled up put it on a very slow fire that
it may do gradually for if the fire is strong the Rice will burn—it
should not be stirred with anything while doing.—When the Rice

---

146. Pasta with a curved, open-bowl shape similar to the bowl of a smoking pipe.
One end is closed where cut from the extruder, while the opposite end remains open
to collect the pasta sauce.

147. Fluffy, long-grain rice grown on Carolina plantations in British Colonial
America. Martha Lloyd was the great-granddaughter of the Honorable C. Craven,
one of the last colonial governors of South Carolina.

is quite tender (which will be in about ~~half~~ an hour & half) take out the Cinamon & Lemon peel, & put in to it a piece of butter about the size of a walnut & a little sugar, work it well with a wooden spoon; when nearly cold build it in your dish about three inches high keeping it smooth outside, & not too thick it may be filled with stewed apple custard or any other stewed fruit.

96

To stew the Apples.

Peel and slice about 14 moderate sized Apples, put into a stew pan a small piece of butter some Lemon peel & cinnamon with the apples; set them over a slow fire 'til quite done & of a reddish color, put some sugar to them, & put it into the Rice, first taking out the cinnamon & Lemon peel, set it in the Oven for ten minutes before sending to table. For a change, whisk the whites of four eggs to a stiff froth, mix with it a little pounded sugar, put it over the apples & strew sugar over it, then put it in the Oven & bake it of a very nice color, send it up quick or the soufflé will fall.

Croquets[148] of Rice are prepared in the same way, only using cream ~~instead~~ in the Rice instead of Butter & one egg well beaten—make them round the size of a croquet, or small apples, egg & bread crum them twice—Either fry or bake them, strew sugar over them & send up quite hot.

---

148. Croquettes: a shaped food, often of ground meat or fish combined with a binding ingredient such as mashed potato, in individual portions, each dipped in egg then covered in breadcrumbs and fried until crisp.

Ginger Beer fit to drink in 24 hours

Two Gallons of Water, 2 oz: cream of Tartar 2 lb lump Sugar 2 lemons sliced, 2 oz ginger bruised, pour the water boiling on the ingredients, then add 2 spoonfuls of good yeast; when cold bottle it in stone bottles and tie the corkes down.

Apple Snow

Core & pare a lb of apples, boil or steam them until tender & put them on a strainer to drain—Add six oz: of fine loaf sugar & two whites of eggs whipt into a froth first by itself—Whip up the apples also separately then put altogether & whisk it up for a full hour until it all looks like snow. —M^rs. Berry

Bread Puddings in cups—

Quarter of a lb of grated bread, quarter lb of butter, quarter of a pint of milk, the butter to be warmed in the milk and mixed first with the bread—add four eggs well beaten, sugar to your taste half a glass of white wine; baked in cups well buttered.

[At this point in the manuscript, the household book was flipped and entries were made from the opposite end towards the centre. This practice separated the cooking recipes from those for cosmetics, household preparations, home remedies and livestock cures. To aid the reader, the transcribed content is sequenced from the back cover towards the centre of the book, replicating the sequence in which the entries were originally made. For ease of reference page numbers have been added to folios originally left unnumbered. These appear in pale type in the margins of the facsimile pages and in square brackets in the transcript.]

[signature inside back cover]

Martha Lloyd

[annotation]

[The index begins on the facing page and continues for two additional pages, which are worn and crumpled along the outside edges. Page numbers that are missing or illegible have been provided from the recipe section.]

[*123*]

[An unnumbered page after the Index is left blank.]

[*122*]

To Make Rasberry Vinegar

Take ripe Rasberries pick'd when quite dry—fill a stone jar with them within 2 Inches of the top—then pour upon them Vinegar sufficent to quite cover them—tye the pot quite close with leather let it stand 12 Days in a dry place. then take off the buff scum, and pour off the liquor quite Clear, by drawing the drugs[149] through a cullender to a pint of Juice add a pound of lump Sugar boil it to a ~~pulp Syrrup Syrup~~ Sirup, keeping it well scum'd, when quite cold put it into bottles tying over them a piece of linnen or pricked paper.

Dr: Molesworth rect[150] for fevers, sore throats—or any small beverage.—in ulcerated sore throats two teaspoonfuls of Brandy to one of Sirup taken ~~two or~~ three or four times a day.

---

149. Dregs.
150. Short for receipt, derived from the Latin *recipere*, meaning to receive or take. In Martha's time, a receipt was both a formula for a medical prescription and a statement of ingredients with instructions for cookery—a recipe.

To cure wounds in Cattle

Three penny-worth of tincture of Myrrh,[151] Four penny-worth of
turpentine,[152] three penny-worth of spirits of wine;[153] mix'd all-
together apply it to the wound.

A certain cure for a swell'd Neck.[154]

[This entry has been crossed through with three large Xs.]
The day the Moon is at full a gentle dose of Salts[155] should be taken,
& then the next day take 20 Grains of burnt spunge[156] (in Honey
Syrop or any thing that will mix it) every Morning fasting till the
Moon changes,[157]

An Easy but certain ~~redemy~~ remedy for a Consumption[158]

Two ounces of the express juice of Hore-hound,[159] mix'd with a pint of
Cow's Milk, and sweeten'd with honey.[160]

---

151. Myrrh resin dissolved in alcohol, believed to rid animals of worms and other
parasites.

152. Distilled tree resin, often taken from live pine trees and used in early home
remedies, most commonly for topical application.

153. A term for any kind of wine distilled, sometimes twice, over a low fire. 'The
slower you distil it the stronger your spirit will be.' (Raffald, *The Experienced English
Housekeeper*, p. 191.) Spirits of wine also had household uses, such as for burning in a
lamp, like kerosene.

154. A goitre, an enlargement of the thyroid gland.

155. A generic term for a variety of medicinal salts, some taken internally for
common complaints such as constipation.

156. Ashes of burnt seaweed, from which iodine is derived.

157. This recipe is repeated and concluded on page [119].

158. A common term for tuberculosis.

159. A flowering plant of the *Lamiaceae* family. The expressed juice was often used in
candy and cough drops.

160. This recipe is repeated on page [119].

Black for Shoes

One Ounces of Gum Dragon[161] dissolv'd in a quart of small Beer wort: add 3 Ounces of Ivory Black.[162] mix it well together, put in a dram[163] [of] Brandy & its fit for Use.

[120]

For the Gravel[164]

One oz: of Marsh Mallow roots,[165] two oz: of pearl barley;[166] put them into 3 pints of water, and boil it to a quart: strain it into a bowl upon an oz: of Gum-arabic,[167] & sweeten it to your taste with honey.—A glass of this to be taken morning & evening.

Remedy for the Hooping Cough[168]

Cut off the hair from the top of the head as large as a Crown piece.[169] Take a piece of brown paper of the same size: dip it in rectified oyl of amber,[170] and apply it to the part[171] for nine Mornings, dipping the

---

161. Tragacanth, the natural gum extracted from any of several species of legumes. The thick, odourless, tasteless gum was used in herbal remedies for common complaints such as coughs and diarrhoea.

162. Granular material produced by charring ivory, used as an artists' pigment.

163. A unit of measure equivalent to one-eighth of an ounce in the old (pre-1864) Apothecaries' System of Weights and Measures.

164. Kidney stones.

165. *Althaea officinalis*, an edible perennial plant with thick, fibrous white roots used in herbal medicines to treat irritations in the mouth and throat. The French confection *pâte de guimauve*, originally made from the root extract, resembled today's commercially prepared marshmallows.

166. Barley grains with the outer hull removed.

167. A natural gum from the hardened sap of the acacia tree, used as a thickening and emulsifying agent.

168. Whooping cough, a bacterial disease characterized by coughing fits; also known as pertussis. Named for the high-pitched whoop sound a person makes when gasping for air.

169. Based on the size of a late Georgian crown coin, roughly 38 mm (or 1½ inches) in diameter.

170. An extract from fossilized tree resin, once used as an analgesic and a sedative.

171. The section of scalp where the hair was removed.

paper fresh every morning. If the Cough is not remov'd try it again after three or four days.—

This medicine is some-times used by rubbing it along the back bone.

[*119*]

A certain cure for a swell'd Neck.

The day the Moon is at full a gentle dose of salts shoud be taken, & then the next day take 20 grains of burnt spunge in honey, syrop, or any thing that will mix it, every morning fasting till the moon changes then take another gentle dose of salts & leave off till the Moon is at full again: & so on for a considerable time till benefit is found.—It is best to buy the spunge at apothecaries Hall[172] & it must be kept very close & dry.

An easy but certain remedy for a consumption.

Two ounces of the expressed juice of Hore hound, mix'd with a pint of new milk, & sweeten'd with Honey.

[*118*]

To make Ink

Take 4 oz: of blue gauls,[173] 2 oz: of green Copperas[174] 1 oz[175] & half of gum Arrabic, break the galls, the gum & Copperas must be beaten in a Mortar & put into a pint of strong stale Beer; with a pint of small

---

172. The London site where the Worshipful Society of Apothecaries manufactured and sold medicinal and pharmaceutical products.

173. Gallic acid, extracted from galls (oak apples), was a key ingredient in writing and drawing ink through the nineteenth century.

174. Iron sulphate, from a range of salts with medicinal, horticultural and industrial uses. The chemical reaction between the iron sulphate and gallotannic acid is the crucial factor for traditional iron gall inks.

175. Presumably an abbreviation for ounce, with a slip of the pen. The entry has been revised; note the ampersand written over the word 'of'.

Beer, put in a little double refin'd Sugar, it must stand in a chimney Corner fourteen days & shaken two or three times a day.

A Cure for Mange[176] in Horses or Dogs

Liver of Antimony[177] & Brimsstone[178] powder'd & equal quantity in weight, mix'd up with lard or Butter to a sufficient consistancy to make into Balls, about the size of a Wallnut; let one be given every morning for three weeks or a month.

    The person who makes them up should rub their hands in flour to prevent its stick[ing.]

[117]

Black for Shoes

One oz: of Gum Dragon disolv'd in a quart of small Beer wort, add 3 oz: of Ivory Black, mix it well together put in a glass of Brandy & it is fit for use.

Eye Water

Two penny-worth of white Copperas,[179] one ditto of Orris root,[180] to be disolved in a quart of spring water. To be shaken when used.

---

    176. A skin disease in animals caused by parasitic mites and characterized by hair loss.

    177. Hepar, a liver-brown-coloured powder formed by heating antimony sulphide with an alkaline sulphide. Often used for treating unhealthy skin conditions.

    178. Ground yellow sulphur powder.

    179. Zinc sulphate. Zinc suphate and iron sulphate were known respectively as white and green copperas.

    180. *Rhizoma iridis*, a root in the iris family once used in medicines but now found primarily in perfumes and potpourri. The root is said to have anti-inflammatory, purgative and diuretic properties. Unlike the iris flower fragrance, the root scent is similar to violets. In culinary use, orris root has the flavour of raspberries.

To make Hard Pomatum[181]

One p^d of Beef Suet, ½ p^d Mutton ditto ½ p^d of Wax, melt them seperately, put them together when nearly cold, an oz: of Essence,[182] pour it into you moulds when ~~near~~ almost cold.—The Suet when melted must be laid in cold water for a week changing it every day.

[*116*]

A good salve for sore Lips

Take an oz:[183] of Bee's-wax; put it into an oz: of good Salad Oyl, melt it over the fire & colour it with Alkany root;[184] when it has boil'd & is of a fine red, strain it and drop in three penny-worth of Balsam of peru,[185] then pour it into the bottom of tea Cups that it may turn out in cakes.   —M^rs. Fowle

To cure worms

Four drams of wallnut leaves dryed & finely powd'rd mix'd up with honey, divide this into eight doses & take one of them Morning & Night for four days successively. The Morning after take for a purge jallap[186] & Rhubarb[187] an equal quantity twenty grains of each for a grown person, to Children in proportion.

To Cure wounds in Cattle

Three penny-worth of tincture of Myrrh, four penny-worth of turpentine, three penny-worth of spirits of wine.

---

181. Pomade, a substance used to style hair and give it a slick or shiny appearance.
182. Referring here to an essential oil with a pleasing fragrance.
183. Presumably an abbreviation for ounce, with a slip of the pen.
184. Alkanet root, a herb in the borage family used as a ruby-red dye.
185. A viscous resin from the balsam tree, used for its fragrance and natural healing properties.
186. Jalap, a tuberous root used as a laxative.
187. Rhubarb plant roots were used in medicine, not the fleshy plant stalks used in cooking.

A Receipt for an Ague[188]

Take 40 Grains of Salt of Tartar[189]

30 Grains of Snake Root[190]

30 G^rs of Salt of Steel[191]

½ an ounce of Bark[192]

Mix them together & divide them into three parts, take one part in a glass of Port wine or Cyder in an hour after the fit is off, & the other in twelve hours after each other. Repeat the same in eight Days after.

A ~~receipt~~ *Salve for Sore eyes*

Take 1 Oz of Butter without Salt half an Oz of white wax 2 drachms[193] of prepared tutty[194] 1 Scruple[195] of Camphire[196] one table spoonful of Rose water let this all simmer a few minutes and stir it till Cold—bind it over the Eye going to bed and wash next Morning with tutty prepared and Elder flower water—May butter[197] is best.

---

188. A severe fever, such as with malaria, marked by recurring periods of chills, fever and sweating.

189. Potassium bitartrate, or cream of tartar, used as a laxative.

190. One of several common names for the plant *Aristolochia serpentaria*, used in folklore and medicine as a remedy for snakebites but now known to be toxic.

191. Sodium sulphate, also known as Glauber's salt, was used as a general-purpose laxative. Discovered by chemist and apothecary Johann Rudolph Glauber in 1625, who called it *sal mirabilis* or miraculous salt.

192. Potentially any of several tree barks with known healing qualities: apple, ash, birch, cedar, elder, elm and others. For example, Peruvian or Jesuit's bark contains quinine, an ingredient in several medicines.

193. Alternate spelling of dram, one-eighth of an ounce.

194. Zinc oxide or cadmium collected from the sides of a smelting furnace and used for skin ulcers and eye diseases.

195. One twenty-fourth of an ounce in the old Apothecaries' System.

196. Camphor, a waxy substance from the camphor laurel tree used topically to treat pain, swelling and inflammation.

197. Butter prepared without salt during the month of May, presumably when cows graze on new grasses. The butter was stored and reserved for medicinal use.

for a pain in the side

Take Honey, and wheat flour mix them well together, the thickness of a salve spread it upon leather. then drop it all over with hartshorn and put it to the side. it must be repeated once in 12 hours till the pain is removed.

for worms

Take cold drawn linced oil.[198] to an infant a Tea spoon a child a pap spoonful[199] a grown person a table spoonful, mix it with treacle. take it 9 mornings[200]

Drink Walnut leave tea Nine Mornings after it [annotation]

[113]

For the Staggers[201]

Cinnabar of Antimony,[202] two drams; Musk[203] half a dram Gum Assafoetida[204] half an ounce, Valerian Root[205] in powder half an Ounce; Winters Bark[206] in powder half an oz; made into a ball with Honey.

---

198. Linseed oil, also known as flaxseed oil, extracted from the ripe seeds of the flax plant and used as a digestive aid.

199. A small spoon with an elongated bowl used to feed soft foods to children, invalids and the elderly.

200. Note that there are other text revisions in this same hand as well as another.

201. A livestock disease characterized by unsteady gait and frequent falls, now thought to be caused by a magnesium deficiency.

202. Mercury sulphide, also known as red cinnabar, once used as the red pigment in cosmetics despite its toxicity being known since ancient times.

203. The dried, paste-like substance obtained from the gland of a male deer. Musk was used to treat strokes, nerve problems and seizures.

204. Gum asafoetida, the dried latex from the rhizome of *Ferula foetida* in the celery family, used here as an antispasmodic. The herb was also used in cooking for its pungent odour and taste described as onion combined with garlic.

205. The roots of the Valerian plant, used as a sedative.

206. *Drimys winteri*, known as winter's bark or canelo, used as a preventative and remedy for scurvy.

Varnish for Tables

Four pennyworth of alkenet root two ditto of rose pink,[207] & one pint of cold drawn Lintseed Oyl.

Lavender Water

To one quart of the best rectified spirits of wine, put three quarters of an oz: of Essence of Lavender & half a scruple of Ambergris;[208] shake it together & it is fit for use in a few days.

To Make a sweet Pot[209]

One pd. of Violets, ½ lb of roses, ¾ of Thyme in bloom, 1½ of sweet marjoram ¾ of a lb of small myrtle, 2 lb of Lavender, ¼ of Rosemary in bloom, ½ qt. of Balm, ⅛ of Bay leaves broke into small pieces, ½ pd. of Pinks, 3 lb of Orange flowers not picked a large quantity of Nutmegs 3 oz: of Cinnamon, 1 oz: of white pepper, the yellow ~~Rhind~~ rind of 4 or 5 lemons grated—The flowers & herbs must be picked clean from the stalks & leaves, & the pinks seperated from their bottoms, the spices must be pounded not too fine.—Then two large handfuls of salt thrown at the bottom of the pot.—Then a layer of flowers & so continue one layer upon another till all the flowers are in—The flowers may be put in as they are fit so as Salt is always thrown in with them, the ingredients should be stirred every day with ~~an~~ wooden spoon, & when the jar is full the spices should be put in & the whole stirred up. It does best when put into a large jar with a good deal of salt & the jar stopp'd close for two or three months. Then put more salt & stir it up well.

---

207. The essence derived from the fragrant flowering plant *Sabatia angularis*, known commonly as rosepink.
208. A waxy substance obtained from the digestive system of a sperm whale, which acquires a sweet, earthy fragrance as it ages.
209. Potpourri.

Coral Tooth Powder[210]

Prepar'd Coral[211]—powder'd.

& Cuttle Fish Bone,[212] powdered, of each one ounce

Rose Pink three Drachms

Powder'd Cassia Bark[213] 2 Drachms

Put all these together in a Mortar

Daffy's Elixer[214]

—M^rs. Davison [illegible annotation]

Senna[215] two oz: Elicampane Guiaxum[216] chip. & Liquirice[217] of each one ounce—Coriander & Cardamum seeds bruised of each a quarter of an ounce,—Raisons stoned a quarter of a pound.

Infuse these ingredients in one quart of best double distilled Anneseed-water[218] for one week, then add one quart of water, stir it every day, & let it stand one week more then strain it through Muslin, & til fit for use.

---

210. A mildly abrasive powder to apply to a moistened toothbrush and used for oral cleansing.

211. Coral calcium powder, used as here in toothpaste and, later, in preparations ranging from bath salts to dental rinses.

212. The porous and calcium-rich internal structure of the cuttlefish.

213. A variety of cinnamon.

214. The name for several different medicines claiming to cure a wide range of disorders. Supposedly developed in 1647 by Leicestershire clergyman Thomas Daffy, the general cure-all was labelled *elixir salutis*, Latin for 'elixir of health'.

215. Derived from the leaves of the *Senna* plant and used as a laxative.

216. Elecampane (an expectorant and diuretic) and Guaiacum (a stimulant).

217. Liquorice is derived from the root of *Glycyrrhiza glabra*, from which a sweet flavouring is extracted.

218. *Aqua anisi*, commonly prescribed in 1-ounce doses as a sleep aid.

For Worms

Rheubarb Powder, Jalap, of each 10 Grains, Calomel[219] prepared 4 Grains. Mix them up with honey. To be taken fasting—The above quantity is for three doses for a Child 4 or five years old, & should be encreased in proportion to its Age. Two or three days between each dose.

[*109*]

Cold Cream

A Dram of Spermacity[220]—A Dram of white Wax—Two Oz: of Oyl of Sweet Almond—An oz. & half of Rose Water.

Rose Pomatum

To a pd. of Roses finely pounded one pd. of Lard, mixed well together, & let stand three days—A small quantity of white Wax, melt it altogether & keep it stirring when it has boiled a few minutes strain it into your pots.

for the cure of the Bite of a Mad Dog

Take the leaves of Rue,[221] picked from the stalks bruised, six ounces. garlick picked from the stalks bruised, Venice treacle[222] & Mithridate[223] and the scraping of pewter, of each four ounces. boil all these over a slow fire, in two quarts of strong ale, till one pint be

---

219. Mercury chloride, initially used as a laxative and a cure-all but later associated with gangrene, gum deterioration and tooth loss.
220. Spermaceti, an oily product from the sperm whale.
221. This bitter culinary herb was sometimes combined with poisonous oleander leaves and used as an ancient cure for snakebites.
222. The common name for *theriaca andromachi*, an exotic blend of sixty-four ingredients (roots, leaves, flowers, seeds, resins, animal parts) pulverized then combined with honey as an antidote for poisonous animal bites.
223. A potion, similar to Venice treacle, used as a universal antidote and as a safeguard against poisons and disease. Attributed to Mithridates VI, king of Pontus in Ancient Greece.

consumed; then strain it, and keep it in a Bottle close stopped, and give of it nine spoonfuls to man or woman Seven mornings fasting, and six to a dog, which will not fail ~~of~~ to effect a cure, if given within nine days, after the biting of the dog. Apply some of the ingredients from which the ~~ingredients from which the~~ liquor was strained to the bitten place.

[108]

Steel Pills

Take of Myrrh one Dram of Salt of ~~Sheel~~ Wormwood[224] half a Dram of Salt of Steal, twelve grains rub them together into a fine powder, then add two spoonfuls of Nutmeg Water, three Drams of Sugar & half a pint of Spring water—Three table spoonfuls to be taken twice in a day—It is better to take made up into Pills.

Camphor Julep[225]

Rub one Dram of Camphor with Three tea spoonfuls of Brandy, add two Drams of Sugar & one pint of boiling water, to onc oz: ~~of~~ & half of the Julep add a tea spoonful of spirit of Lavender—two large table spoonfuls is an oz:—The Camphor being a resin, never thoroughly dissolves pounding it & rubbing it in two or three spoonfuls of Brandy is the best method—it may be strained or not as most agreeable.

[107]

Rose Pomatum

Take a sufficient quantity of Lard of the best kind put it into a deep pan and stir in with a wooden spoon a quantity of Rose Leaves, putting in a few at a time Cover it over with a Cloth and let it stand all night for ten days keep adding Rose Leaves putting in the

---

224. Potassium carbonate, obtained from the ashes of wormwood and used for digestive complaints and other ailments.

225. A beverage combining alcohol (such as brandy) and sugar, often accented with a herb.

yellow that is in the centre of the flower, the first day put a sufficient quantity of salt in to keep the Lard sweet & at the end of ten days put your Pomatum into a Kettle of water—Put this on the fire & let it simmer for three hours then squeeze as much as possible from the Rose Leaves, thro a fine piece of Cloth take off the cake putting it into a wide pan, When quite cold take off the cake & throw away the liquor, continue to melt it in the same way till all the Liquor is seperated from the Pomatum—Put it into Pots and keep it at least three four months, it will be still better at the end of six Months, in order to make the Pomatum of a proper consistency it will be necessary to add when melting a sufficient quantity of Mutton suet the quantity of Suet must be regulated by the time of year it is to be used in.

[*106*]

Tincture of Guaiacum

2 oz of Powder of Guaiacum[226] in a pint of Brandy to stand till it is clear

[*105*]

Soap for the Hands

Take of soft soap one p^d. Spermaceti three ounces. dissolve in a water bath—add Camphor in powder one ounce—mix by stirring it well together.

---

226. Derived from a flowering plant in the caltrop family, used to treat syphilis and as a stimulant, particularly to encourage menstruation.

A Wash for Rooms[227]

2 oz: of Indigo[228] well ground

7 p^ds: of London Whiting[229]

1 lb of Glue

Boil the Glue in 9 pints of Water as a size, then add your other ingredients to it, which should be ~~drawn~~ used cold & if made some days previously it is the better—To Wash the Rooms Buff[230] instead of Blue, substitute dutch Pink & Spruce Ocre. N:B: If done upon Wainscoat the Size to be rather stronger of the Glue[231]

[*104*]

For a Fever

2 Grains of Tartar Emetic[232] in an oz of Water—a desert spoonful to be given to a child every two hours 'till it operates or till all is taken, The Child who takes this quantity should be not less than three years old.

Pot-pouri

Gather your Roses free from Wet & dry them in a shady Room, & Lavender when quite ripe the same. When they are perfectly dry they must be put into a Jar with a qarter or half a p^d: of orris powder[233] according to the quantity of Roses. Half an oz: of Benjamin[234] & half

---

227. Indicating a wash of colour as opposed to a cleansing wash.

228. Indigo blue dye, made from the plant *Indigofera tinctoria*, was one of the primary goods imported to Britain by the East India Trading Company.

229. Powdered white chalk that was used in whitewash or added to other paint to increase opacity.

230. Buff indicated a neutral beige colour with a yellow-pink cast.

231. Probably meaning that if the wash were to be used on wooden wall panelling, the proportion of glue would need to be increased to bind it to the wood.

232. Antimony potassium tartrate, a powerful and toxic compound used in minute quantities to induce vomiting.

233. Dried and pounded orris root derived from varieties of iris flowers. Used in medicine as well as a fixative and lasting or base note in potpourris.

234. Probably a corrupted pronunciation of 'benzoin', a balsamic resin obtained from the bark of *Styrax* trees, used in perfumes and incense. It has a strong scent,

an oz: of stora,[235] some Cloves pounded, some Cinnamon, cover it & ~~stirred~~ stir it now & then—

Put any perfume you like on a bit of cotton, & <u>when dry</u> put it with the rest into sweet Bags.

[103]

D^r: Turton's receipt for a Cold

Take volatile salt of Armoniac[236] 32 G^{rs}:—Salt ~~of~~ petre 40 G^{rs}: rub them on a Marble Mortar to a a fine powder, then add one oz: of Syrup of Balsam[237] & one oz: of oyl of sweet Almonds, add six oz: of pump Water. The whole of the above will make four draughts,[238] one of which should be taken three times in 24 hours, & to the night one add one Dram of Elixir of Paragoria.[239]

To whiten Silk Stockings

When they are washed take a table or stool, turn it bottom upwards, then make it close with a sheet, pin the stockings round the in side, take a chaffing dish with Charcoal, break stone Brimsstone & strew over it, then cover it close & it will make them white.

To make Camphire Julep.

One D^{rm} of Camphire, add a pint of Boiling Water, then put a q^r. of an Oz. of Spirit of Lavendar, & one hundred & twenty drops of Tincture of Castor.[240] A small Wine glass for a dose. Rub the Camphire with a little Brandy, or Spirit of Wine.   —Miss Debary

---

reminiscent of vanilla and balsam.

235. Storax, a fragrant balsam obtained from tree bark. It is distinct from benzoin.
236. Sal ammoniac, a naturally occurring white salt used as an anti-inflammatory.
237. Resin from the tolu balsam tree, used in cough syrup.
238. Doses of liquid.
239. Paragoric elixir, a household remedy including anise seed oil, powdered opium and camphor, was widely used as a pain reliever, expectorant and to treat diarrhoea.
240. Castor oil, made from pressed beans of the castor plant and used as a laxative.

The Black Plaister[241]

Take of the best Oyl one pint, of the best red lead[242] half a p^d: of the best white lead a quarter of a p^d:, boil these for a while continually stirring it: then add two oz: of the best Bee's wax, & then boil it again till it is very brown, then rub a board with a with a little Oyl & let it cool & so rub it on the board & make it up in Rolls for use.

If you design it for sear[243] cloth's add to it one oz: of Castile Soap.[244]

—M^rs. Raymond

Carmine Powder[245] & Flannel to clean Gilt things[246] <u>not</u> the dead Gold.[247] [annotation]

Milk of Roses[248]

—Cap^n. Austen

½ Pint of Rose Water—½ an oz: of Oil of Sweet Almonds—12 Grains of salt of Tartar—To be mixed well altogether.

Cold Cream

—L^y. Bridges

45 Grains of White Wax, 1 D^m. ½ of Spermaceti, 2 oz: of Oil of sweet Almonds, mixt well together & beat up with Rose water to a fine Cream

---

241. A protective dressing for wounds.
242. Common lead-based paint pigment, now known to be toxic.
243. Cerecloth, a protective covering for wounds and bruises made from linen or other fabric coated with melted wax. From Latin *cera*, meaning wax.
244. A hard, olive oil-based soap originating from the Castile region of Spain.
245. Powder formed from dried and pounded cochineal insects.
246. Any items with a thin layer of gold or gold leaf.
247. Brass, commonly used for utilitarian household wares such as candlesticks, bowls and pots.
248. A cosmetic lotion purported to clear and preserve the skin.

Black Draught

—M^rs. E: Knight

One oz of Senna 1½ do of Epsom Salts[249] ¼ of an oz of Manna,[250] ¼ of an oz: of Cloves—The whole to be boiled ten minutes and to be divided into three doses to each dose add a desert spoonful of Brandy.

Saline draft

Dissolve 25 grams of carbonate of Soda[251] in three table spoonsful of Camphor Julep, add one table spoonful of Lemon juice, a little sugar, & drink it whilst in a state of fermentation[252] or not as most agreeable.

—M^r. Jenkins. 1829

For the tooth ach

Opium in the gross purified; an equal quantity of Camphor, make it into a pill, being moistened with Spirits of wine, to the size proper for the tooth to receive it—If the first does not give ease in the course of half an hour, apply a second in its room.[253]

—M^rs. S: Terry

---

249. i.e. 1½ oz. of Epsom salts, or magnesium sulphate, used here as a laxative.

250. Extract of the manna plant, *Fraxinus ornus*, used as a laxative and an expectorant.

251. Sodium carbonate, an alkaline salt that produces a cooling and fizzing sensation. Also used in sherbet powder because it produces its fizzing reaction when mixed with saliva.

252. Referring here to the fizzing of the active ingredient.

253. i.e. in its place.

Apperient[254] Mixture

—D*r*. Hortigan

Sulphate of Magnesia[255] two oz:, Water one pint & half, Tincture of Senna one oz: Mix these together, Take a ~~Table Spoonful~~ Tea Cup full more or less occasionally as required.

Bark Mixture

—D*r*. Hortigan

Take half an oz of coarsely powdered Bark,[256] pour upon it half a pint of Boiling Water—Let it stand three Hours, pour it off & add half an oz of Cardamum Tincture,[257] & two Spoonsful of Elixir of Vitriol[258]—A Table spoonful to be taken three times in a day.

100 [*inverted*]

Blacking[259]

—C. Dexter Esq*r*

One quarter of a p*d*. of Ivory Black—¼ lb Molasses or <u>course</u> brown sugar, one table spoonful of oil of Vitriol—One table spoonful of sweet Oil—one pint of Beer—two wine glasses of Vinegar & as much prussian blue[260] as will lie on a six pence[261]

---

254. A general term for various medicinal preparations used to relieve constipation.

255. Magnesium sulphate, used here as a laxative.

256. Potentially any of several tree barks with known healing qualities: apple, ash, birch, cedar, elder, elm and others. For example, Peruvian or Jesuit's bark contains quinine, an ingredient in several medicines.

257. Derived from the cardamom plant and used to treat mild colic, flatulence, nausea and gastric disorders.

258. A mixture of sulphuric acid and alcohol used to treat scurvy.

259. Shoe polish.

260. A dark blue pigment used in paints and dyes, first synthesized in the eighteenth century.

261. Based on the diameter of a late Georgian sixpence (21 mm or $^{7}/_{8}$ inch), roughly ¼ tsp.

For cleaning Silks & Gauzes

Mix well together 6 oz: of honey, 4 oz: of soft Soap until it becomes a kind of paste, then dissolve it in half a pint of strong Whiskey or hollands[262] & spread your handkerchiefs on a clean Table & rub it well with a soft brush, when it has sufficiently imbibed the mixture rince it in several waters but be careful neither to wring or squeese it; hang it up to drope[263] but not in the air; when half dry shake it well & mangle or iron it. For Gauze, add a little honey or white sugar in the last rinsing water.

99 [inverted]

262. Hollands, also called Hollands Gin, a juniper-based mash originally made in Holland.
263. Drip.

The kitchen at Chawton Cottage as seen today by visitors to Jane Austen's House in Hampshire. The original open hearth was upgraded with an iron range some time before 1809.

Glossary

Many of the following terms are listed as they appear in *Martha Lloyd's Household Book*. Modern spellings are provided to help the reader. Note that many period recipes, both culinary and medicinal, contain ingredients now known to be toxic and are not advised for consumption or use.

ANGELICA—*Angelica archangelica*, a sweetly scented herb with lacy white flowers and hollow stems, known commonly as wild celery. Both the stems and flowers are edible and can be prepared as candy and cake decorations.

ANNESEED-WATER—*Aqua anisi* or anise seed water, commonly prescribed in 1 ounce doses as a sleep aid.

APOTHECARIES' HALL—The London site where the Worshipful Society of Apothecaries manufactured and sold medicinal and pharmaceutical products.

APRICOT KERNEL—The seed found inside the stone of the apricot fruit. Ground apricot kernels were used in confections and liquors, but are now known to be toxic.

BARK—Potentially any of several tree barks with known healing qualities: apple, ash, birch, cedar, elder, elm and others. For example, Peruvian or Jesuit's bark contains quinine, an ingredient in several medicines.

BARM—The yeasty scum or foam that forms on top of the brew.

BRINE—A salty pickling liquid. Occasionally, a period recipe called for brine thick enough 'to bear an egg', meaning one made salty enough for an egg to float in it.

BUTTER SAUCE—Also referred to as 'melted butter' in period recipes, 'butter sauce' usually indicates a butter-and-water mixture thickened with flour. If the sauce is overheated in the early stages, the mixture will 'oil', or separate. It is rare that a recipe would instruct a cook simply to melt fresh butter on its own.

CAMPHOR OR CAMPHIRE—A waxy substance from the camphor laurel tree used topically to treat pain, swelling and inflammation.

CATCHUP—A thick condiment sauce. Unlike modern ketchup, eighteenth-century ketchups were not tomato-based.

COMMON SALT—Coarse salt or kitchen salt.

CONSUMPTION—A common term for tuberculosis.

CREAM OF TARTAR—Potassium bitartrate, the crystals that form as grapes ferment in the wine-making process. When used in home brewing, cream of tartar helps break up and stabilize sugar. Also known as salt of tartar and used as a laxative.

CULLENDER—Variant spelling of colander.

DRACHM or DRAM—A unit of measure equivalent to ⅛ ounce in the old (pre-1864) Apothecaries' System of Weights and Measures.

DRAUGHT—In medicinal terms, a dose of liquid.

DUTCH OVEN—A term referring to two different cooking tools: (1) A semi-circular sheet of reflective metal placed hearthside behind food to brown it. This was also called a reflecting oven, reflecting pan or hastener. At some point the sheet was fitted with a spit for roasting joints of meat, similar to today's rotisserie. (2) A cooking pot with thick sides and a tight-fitting lid, most commonly of cast iron. Hot coals from the fire were placed on the pot's flat lid to raise the temperature and cook the food within.

FEEDING SUGAR—Inexpensive brown sugar, sometimes used to fatten livestock, especially pigs.

FISH SAUCE—A popular condiment, most often fermented, for use on fish, seafood or meats. Mixed with butter, it made a flavourful addition to cooked vegetables. Compares with Worcestershire sauce.

FLITCH—One side of a butchered pig that has been split in half.

FORCE MEAT—Ground meat or sausage, from the French *farcir*, to stuff; it could also refer to meatballs or patties.

GRAIN—A unit of measure equivalent to $\frac{1}{20}$ scruple or $\frac{1}{60}$ drachm in the Apothecaries' System of Weights and Measures.

GUAIACUM—Derived from a flowering plant in the caltrop family, used to treat syphilis and as a stimulant, particularly to encourage menstruation.

GUM ARABIC—A natural gum from the hardened sap of the acacia tree, used as a thickening and emulsifying agent.

GUM DRAGON—Tragacanth, the natural gum extracted from any of several species of legumes. The thick, odourless, tasteless gum was used in herbal remedies for common complaints such as coughs and diarrhoea.

HARTSHORN—Obtained from the antlers of a male red deer; used culinarily in either shaved or powdered form. The heat-activated hartshorn worked as a thickening agent with leavening properties similar to today's baking ammonia or baking powder.

HAIR SIEVE—A straining device formed from a wooden hoop with closely strung horsehair.

HOCKS—Also known as pork knuckles, the joint of a butchered pig between the leg and the foot.

HOREHOUND—A flowering plant of the *Lamiaceae* family. The expressed juice was often used in candy and cough drops.

ISINGLASS—A powdery gelling agent made from fish bladders that have been dried and pounded. Compares with today's gelatin.

IVORY BLACK—Granular material produced by charring ivory, used as an artists' pigment.

JALAP—A tuberous root used as a laxative.

JELLY BAG—A canvas or muslin bag used to strain fruit solids from the liquids. Typically used in the jelly-making process but also used in other culinary applications.

JULEP—A beverage combining alcohol (such as brandy) and sugar, often accented with a herb.

LAWN SIEVE—A straining or sifting device made from a wooden band or hoop strung with closely placed material to form a mesh.

LINSEED OIL—Also known as flaxseed oil, the extract from the ripe seeds of the flax plant, used as a digestive aid.

LIQUOR—The liquid resulting from a cooking process, such as drippings or broth from roasted or baked meats; also the juice from mashed or strained fruit.

LISBON SUGAR—Lisbon in Portugal produced what was considered the finest quality loaf sugar available. Many recipes dating from the mid-eighteenth century call for Lisbon sugar specifically.

LOAF SUGAR—White or refined sugar was purchased in large cones commonly called loaves. A typical family-sized loaf of sugar weighed between 11 and 13 pounds. The cook used sugar nippers or a sugar hammer to break the loaf into smaller pieces or lumps. For fine granules, the cook pounded the lumps in a mortar with a pestle.

LONG PEPPER—The dried immature fruits of the flowering vine *Piper longum* or *Piper retrofractum*, with a taste similar to but hotter than black peppercorns.

MACE—A spice made from the dried and ground outer membrane of nutmeg. Mace has a pungent, earthy flavour and was used frequently in eighteenth-century dishes.

MEAD—A fermented beverage of ancient origin, made from honey.

MORTAR AND PESTLE—A small, heavy work bowl and hand-held grinding tool with a rounded end, often made of marble, for culinary or medicinal use. These could also be made of wood, although less durable and prone to absorb oils and other liquids.

MOUNTAIN—Also known as Mountain wine, a sweet wine from the hills around Malaga, Spain, that was popular in the late eighteenth and early nineteenth centuries.

MYRRH—Myrrh resin dissolved in alcohol as a tincture was believed to rid animals of worms and other parasites.

ORANGE FLOWER WATER—An aromatic flavouring distilled from fresh bitter-orange blossoms.

ORANGE PEEL—Usually refers to candied orange peel for confectionary use. Made from narrow strips of peel that have been boiled in sugar syrup then air-dried until crisp.

PASTE—Pastry crust, or what we would now call shortcrust or piecrust pastry.

PECK—A unit of dry measure equivalent to one-fourth of a bushel or 2 gallons.

POMATUM—Pomade, a substance used to style hair and give it a slick or shiny appearance.

POTTED MEAT—Meats preserved with layers of fat and spices and stored in heavy earthenware pots.

PUDDING—This often referred to a soft dough, often made with suet, rolled and tied in a cloth and boiled in water until cooked through. Puddings could be sweet or savoury.

PUFF PASTE—A light and flaky pastry made from compressed layers of dough and butter; now referred to as puff pastry.

RACE-GINGER—Root ginger, used fresh in both sweet and savoury dishes. The pounded yellow flesh added a sweetly pungent taste. The dried powdered root was also used in eighteenth-century cooking to provide a more fiery taste.

RECEIPT—A term used for both a formula for a medical prescription and a statement of ingredients with instructions for cookery—what we would now call a recipe. Derived from the Latin *recipere*, meaning 'to receive' or 'to take'.

RICE FLOUR—A thickening agent made from rice that has been parched, beaten and sieved to create a fine flour.

ROSE PINK—The essence derived from the fragrant flowering plant *Sabatia angularis*, known commonly as rosepink.

SACK—A fortified white wine from mainland Spain or the Canary Islands. Compares with today's sherry.

SALAMANDER—A long rod with a flat iron plate at one end that is thrust into the fire until red hot then suspended over food to brown it.

SALT OF TARTAR *see* cream of tartar

SALTPETRE—Potassium nitrate, a naturally occurring chemical compound used in food preservation. When used to cure meats, it reacts with haemoglobin to create a pink colour.

SALTS—A generic term for a variety of medicinal salts, some taken internally for common complaints such as constipation.

SCRUPLE—A unit of measurement equivalent to ⅓ drachm or 1/24 ounce in the old Apothecaries' System.

SENNA—Derived from the leaves of the senna plant and used as a laxative.

SEVILLE ORANGES—Tart, nubby-skinned oranges from Seville in Spain, available in the UK for a three-month period, generally December to February.

SMALL BEER—Beer with a low alcohol content. An acceptable beverage for families and servants because several glasses could be consumed without causing intoxication.

SPERMACETI—An oily product from the sperm whale used in cold cream and hand soap.

SPIRITS OF WINE—A term for any kind of wine distilled, sometimes twice, over a low fire. Spirits of wine also had household uses, such as for burning in a lamp, similar to kerosene.

SUET—The hard fat located around the kidneys and loins of beef or mutton, used raw. Suet was a staple ingredient in both sweet and savoury puddings.

SUGAR CANDY—Drops or sticks of sugar candy, sometimes made with fruit or other flavourings.

SULPHATE OF MAGNESIA—Magnesium sulphate, used as a laxative. Also known as Epsom salts.

SWEETBREADS—The general term for either the thymus (gullet, throat or neck sweetbread) or the pancreas (belly, stomach or gut sweetbread) glands of calf or lamb.

SWEETMEATS—Any confectionary variety of sweets such as candied fruits, caramelized nuts, bonbons, sugarplums or other candy.

SWELLED NECK—The common term for a goitre.

SYLLABUB—A froth of whipped cream curdled with an acid (e.g. lemon or orange juice), sweetened with sugar and flavoured with alcohol (e.g. wine or sherry).

TREACLE—Black treacle, like molasses, is formed during the sugar refining process, when sugar cane juice has been boiled down.

TUN—A wine or beer cask. Tunning refers to a step in the brewing or winemaking process when the brew or wine is poured into a cask.

TURPENTINE—Distilled tree resin, often taken from live pine trees and used in early home remedies, most commonly for topical application.

WIGS—Light, fluffy buns made with milk or cream, often with seeds such as caraway.

WORT—The liquid extracted after grains are mashed during the brewing process. The wort contains sugars that feed the yeast and lead to fermentation, producing alcohol.

Notes

FOREWORD

1. *Jane Austen's Letters*, ed. Deirdre Le Faye, 4th edn, Oxford University Press, Oxford, 2011, p. 17.
2. Ibid., p. 20.
3. Ibid., p. 119.
4. Ibid., p. 126.
5. Ibid., p. 119.
6. Ibid., p. 336.

PREFACE

1. *Jane Austen's Letters*, ed. Deirdre Lc Faye, 4th edn, Oxford University Press, Oxford, 2011, p. 199.

MARTHA LLOYD IN HER OWN LIGHT

1. Parody of 'Which of all my important nothings shall I tell you first?' (15 June 1808), in *Jane Austen's Letters*, ed. Deirdre Le Faye, 4th edn, Oxford University Press, Oxford, 2011, p. 130. (Henceforth *Letters*.)
2. 29 November 1812, in *Letters*, p. 204.
3. Caroline Mary Craven Austen, *Reminiscences of Caroline Austen*, intro. and ed. Deirdre Le Faye, Jane Austen Society, Jane Austen's House Museum, Chawton, Hampshire, 2004, pp. 3–7.
4. Ibid., pp. 74–6.
5. Caroline Austen, *Reminiscences*, p. 7. Martha's niece Caroline wrote that a Welshman and a scholar convinced her that it was useless to try to imitate the Welsh pronunciation with an English tongue, so she had better say 'Lloyd'.
6. Deirdre Le Faye, *A Chronology of Jane Austen and Her Family: 1600–2000*, Cambridge University Press, Cambridge, 2006, p. 283. In Revd John Craven's will, he made a small bequest to his sister 'Martha Floyd'.
7. Caroline Austen, *Reminiscences*, pp. 7–11.
8. Le Faye, *A Chronology*, p. 172.
9. Ibid., p. 194.
10. Deirdre Le Faye, *Jane Austen: A Family Record*, Cambridge University Press, Cambridge, 2004, pp. 68–9.

11. Jane Austen, *Minor Works*, ed. R.W. Chapman, Oxford University Press, Oxford, 1988, p. 3.
12. 18 September 1796, in *Letters*, p. 13.
13. 26 December 1798, in *Letters*, p. 32.
14. 30 November 1800, in *Letters*, pp. 67–8.
15. Le Faye, *Jane Austen: A Family Record*, p. 99.
16. 27 October 1798, in *Letters*, p. 17.
17. 19 December 1798, in *Letters*, p. 28.
18. 24 December 1798, in *Letters*, p. 30.
19. 9 January 1799, in *Letters*, p. 35.
20. 11 June 1799, in *Letters*, p. 46.
21. 9 January 1799, in *Letters*, p. 35.
22. Le Faye, *Jane Austen: A Family Record*, p. 128.
23. Le Faye, *A Chronology*, p. 252.
24. Ibid., p. 257.
25. Ibid., p. 261.
26. 22 May 1801, in *Letters*, p. 92.
27. Caroline Austen, *Reminiscences*, pp. 2–3.
28. Le Faye, *A Chronology*, p. 308.
29. 9 April 1805, in *Letters*, p. 104.
30. *Jane Austen: Collected Poems and Verse of the Austen Family*, ed. David Selwyn, Jane Austen Society and Fyfield Books, Manchester, 1996, pp. 20–21.
31. 21 April 1805, in *Letters*, p. 109.
32. Le Faye, *A Chronology*, p. 229.
33. Ibid., p. 328.
34. Ibid., p. 330.
35. Richard's Pills were taken to improve general circulation and as a specific treatment for male impotence.
36. Morton's wife probably refers to William Morton's wife Louisa. The Mortons were friends of Martha Lloyd and lived in Masham, a village roughly 18 miles north of the spa town of Harrogate in North Yorkshire.
37. *Jane Austen: Collected Poems and Verse*, pp. 5–6.
38. Le Faye, *Jane Austen: A Family Record*, p. 153.
39. 8 February 1807, in *Letters*, p. 123.
40. 22 February 1807, in *Letters*, p. 129.
41. Robin Vick, 'A tourist's view of Southampton and Portsmouth in 1811', in *Collected Reports 1996–2000*, Jane Austen Society, Bristol, 2005, p. 38.
42. 9 October 1808, in *Letters*, p. 151.
43. 21 February 1807, in *Letters*, p. 128.
44. 7 October 1808, in *Letters*, p. 149.
45. 1–2 October 1808, in *Letters*, p. 147.
46. 13 October 1808, in *Letters*, p. 152.
47. 1 October 1808, in *Letters*, pp. 146–7.
48. 20 November 1808, in *Letters*, p. 161.
49. 9 December 1808, in *Letters*, p. 163.
50. 27–8 December 1808, in *Letters*, pp. 166–8.
51. Le Faye, *A Chronology*, p. 613.
52. 29 November 1812, in *Letters*, pp. 204–5.

53. 29 November 1812, in *Letters*, p. 205.
54. 26 November 1815, in *Letters*, p. 313.
55. Le Faye, *A Chronology*, p. 450.
56. 20 November 1814, in *Letters*, p. 293.
57. 6 June 1811, in *Letters*, p. 202.
58. 29 November 1812, in *Letters*, p. 205.
59. 29 January 1813, in *Letters*, p. 211.
60. Caroline Austen, *Reminiscences*, p. 46.
61. 23 June 1814, in *Letters*, pp. 276–7.
62. Le Faye, *A Chronology*, pp. 545–6.
63. Ibid., p. 563.
64. 22 May 1817, in *Letters*, p. 357.
65. Deirdre Le Faye, 'To dwell together in unity', in *Collected Reports 1986–1995*, Jane Austen Society, Alton, 1997, p. 158.
66. Le Faye, *A Chronology*, p. 634.
67. Ibid., p. 635.
68. Ibid.
69. David Hopkinson, 'The Later Life of Sir Francis Austen', in *Collected Reports 1976–1985*, Jane Austen Society, Overton, 1989, p. 255.
70. Martha Austen (née Lloyd) to Revd J.E. Austen, Tring Park, Hertfordshire, Collection of Freydis Welland, Gosport, 30 September 1828.
71. Le Faye, *A Chronology*, p. 636.
72. Ibid., p. 638.
73. Ibid., p. 640.
74. Ibid., p. 641.
75. Ibid., pp. 666–7.
76. *Collected Reports 1976–1985*, p. 254.
77. Le Faye, *A Chronology*, p. 641.
78. *Family Record*, p. 268.
79. Le Faye, *A Chronology*, pp. 650–51.
80. Ibid., p. 655.
81. *Collected Reports 1976–1985*, p. 256.
82. Le Faye, *A Chronology*, p. 658.
83. Deirdre Le Faye, 'Anna Lefroy and Her Austen Family Letters', *Princeton University Library Chronicle*, vol. 62, no. 3, Spring 2001, p. 552.
84. Le Faye, *A Chronology*, p. 663.
85. Le Faye, 'Anna Lefroy and Her Austen Family Letters', pp. 554–5.
86. Le Faye, *A Chronology*, p. 663.
87. Ibid., p. 667.
88. Ibid., pp. 677–8.
89. *Collected Reports 1976–1985*, p. 256.
90. 30 November 1800, in *Letters*, p. 66.
91. 15 October 1808, in *Letters*, p. 153.
92. George Holbert Tucker, 'Jane Austen's Topaz Cross', *Collected Reports 1976–1985*, Jane Austen Society, Overton, 1989, pp. 76–7.
93. *Collected Reports 1986–1995*, p. 161.

1. James Woodforde, *A Country Parson: James Woodforde's Diary 1759–1802*, Tiger Books, London, 1991, p. 187.
2. Nicola Lillie and Marilyn Yurdan, *Lavender Water & Snail Syrup: Miss Ambler's Household Book of Georgian Cures and Remedies*, The History Press, Stroud, 2013, pp. 9–27.
3. Gervase Markham, *The English Huswife*, Roger Jackson, London, 1615, title page.
4. *The Whole Duty of a Woman*, *c.* 1700, British Library Digital Store 14477.a.38, p. 174.
5. 30 August 1805, in *Jane Austen's Letters*, ed. Deirdre Le Faye, 4th edn, Oxford University Press, Oxford, 2011, p. 117. Jane references Thomas Gisborne's *An Enquiry into the Duties of the Female Sex*, stating that she had originally determined not to read the book but is now pleased with it.
6. Lillie and Yurdan, *Lavender Water & Snail Syrup*, p. 24.
7. Susanna Whatman, *The Housekeeping Book of Susanna Whatman 1776–1800*, Random Century and National Trust, London, 1987, pp. 37–54.
8. Belinda Montagu, *To the Manor Born: Lady Montagu of Beaulieu*, Gentry Books, London, 1971, pp. 6–10.
9. Knight Family, *The Knight Family Cookbook*, *c.* 1793, Chawton House, Chawton, Hampshire.
10. John Bell, *A New Catalogue of Bell's Circulating Library*, J. Bell, London, 1774; John Boosey, *A New Catalogue of the Circulating Library at No. 39, King Street, Cheapside*, John Boosey, London, 1787.
11. Deirdre Le Faye, *A Chronology of Jane Austen and Her Family: 1600–2000*, Cambridge University Press, Cambridge, 2006, p. 218.
12. Hannah Glasse, *The Art of Cookery Made Plain and Easy*, E. and J. Exshaw, Dublin, 1748, p. 288.
13. Charlotte Mason, *The Lady's Assistant for Regulating and Supplying the Table*, J. Walter, London, 1787, p. 311.
14. Elizabeth Raffald, *The Experienced English Housekeeper*, R. Baldwin, London, 1786, p. 85.
15. Julienne Gehrer, *Dining with Jane Austen*, Ash Grove Press, Prairie Village KS, 2019, p. 11.
16. Carolyn Shaw, *Cooks and Quakers: 200 Years of a Family's Recipe Books*, Quacks Books, York, 2016, p. 5.
17. Jervoise Family of Herriard estate and personal accounts, *c.* 1660s–1720s, Hampshire Record Office, Winchester, 44M69/E7/55.
18. Stewardship accounts for the estate of Edward Austen, later Edward Knight esquire, 1809–1819, Bradley Trimmer of Alton, solicitors, Hampshire Record Office, Winchester, 79M78/B211.
19. Virginia Mescher, '"How Sweet It Is!" A History of Sugar and Sugar Refining in the United States', 2005, Ragged Soldier, raggedsoldier.com/sugar_history.pdf (accessed 11 May 2019).

UNIQUE DETAILS OF MARTHA'S BOOK

1. Letter from R.M. Mowll to R.W. Chapman, 7 September 1953, T.E. Carpenter Letters Archive Number 1351, Jane Austen's House.
2. Ronald Dunning, 'Jane Austen's Family', 2017, RootsWeb, wc.rootsweb.com/trees/153642/I18/-/descendancy (accessed 27 August 2019).

3. Letter from R.W. Chapman to T. Edward Carpenter, 9 September 1953, T.E. Carpenter Letters Archive Number 1353.
4. *Jane Austen: Collected Poems and Verse of the Austen Family*, ed. David Selwyn, Jane Austen Society and Fyfield Books, Manchester, 1996, pp. 32–3.
5. R.M. Mowll to T. Edward Carpenter, 15 October 1953, Carpenter Letters Archive Number 1401.
6. R.M. Mowll to T. Edward Carpenter, 7 January 1956, Carpenter Letters Archive Number 2408. In addition to Martha's Lloyd's cookery book, Mrs Mowll made reference in other correspondence to owning a manuscript of *Love and Friendship*. This is actually *Volume the Second*, a notebook of Jane Austen's teenage writings, now in the collection of the British Library. Mrs Mowell also owned Jane Austen's copy of her letter including a poem written to Francis Austen (dated 26 July 1809), plus a copy of *The Minstrel* by James Beattie inscribed 'M. Lloyd The gift of her nephew J.E. Austen 1826'. These items were eventually sold to the Jane Austen Memorial Trust. Separately, Mrs Mowll sold to the JAMT a handkerchief embroidered by Jane Austen for her sister Cassandra, and a letter of invitation to Francis Austen to the investiture of the Order of the Bath.
7. R.M. Mowll to T. Edward Carpenter, 7 January 1956, Carpenter Letters Archive Number 2408.
8. R.M. Mowll to T. Edward Carpenter, 30 May 1956, Carpenter Letters Archive Number 2568.
9. R.M. Mowll to T. Edward Carpenter, 4 June 1956, Carpenter Letters Archive Number 2582.
10. W.A. Churchill, *Watermarks in Paper in Holland, England, France, etc., in the XVII and XVIII Centuries and Their Interconnection*, Menno Hertzberger, Amsterdam, 1935, p. 28.
11. Ibid., pp. 43–4.
12. Nicola Lillie and Marilyn Yurdan, *Lavender Water & Snail Syrup: Miss Ambler's Household Book of Georgian Cures and Remedies*, The History Press, Stroud, 2013, pp. 46, 98.
13. Deirdre Le Faye, *A Chronology of Jane Austen and her Family: 1600–2000*, Cambridge University Press, Cambridge, 2006.
14. *Jane Austen's Letters*, ed. Deirdre Le Faye, 4th edn, Oxford University Press, Oxford, 2011.
15. Deirdre Le Faye, *Jane Austen: A Family Record*, Cambridge University Press, Cambridge, 2004, p. 99.
16. *Jane Austen's Later Manuscripts*, ed. Janet Todd and Linda Bree, Cambridge University Press, Cambridge, 2008, p. 705.
17. 25 November 1798, in *Letters*, p. 22.
18. Peggy Hickman, *A Jane Austen Household Book*, David & Charles, North Pomfret VT, 1977, pp. 69–70.
19. Austen-Leigh Family: Diary Kept by Mary Austen, 1836, Hampshire Record Office, Winchester, 23M93/62/1/17.
20. Belinda Montagu, *To the Manor Born: Lady Montagu of Beaulieu*, Gentry Books, London, 1971, p. 102.
21. Hickman, *A Jane Austen Household Book*, p. 37.

1. 24 January 1817, in *Jane Austen's Letters*, ed. Deirdre Le Faye, 4th edn, Oxford University Press, Oxford, 2011, p. 342. (Henceforth *Letters*.)
2. 14 January 1796, in *Letters*, p. 4.
3. *Pride and Prejudice*, vol. 2 of *The Novels of Jane Austen*, 6 vols, ed. R.W. Chapman, Oxford University Press, Oxford, 1988, p. 55.
4. *The Knight Family Cookbook*, *c.* 1793, Chawton House Library, Chawton, Hampshire, p. 197.
5. *Emma*, vol. 4 of *The Novels of Jane Austen*, p. 298.
6. Ibid., p. 218.
7. *Pride and Prejudice*, p. 35.
8. Ibid., p. 342.
9. 17 November 1798, in *Letters*, p. 20.
10. Gervase Markham, *The English Huswife*, Roger Jackson, London, 1615, p. 128.
11. 1 December 1798, in *Letters*, p. 24.
12. *Lesley Castle*, vol. 6 of *The Novels of Jane Austen*, p. 113.
13. Martha Lloyd, *Martha Lloyd's Household Book*, *c.* 1796, Jane Austen's House, Chawton, Hampshire, p. 35.
14. *Mansfield Park*, vol. 3 of *The Novels of Jane Austen*, p. 31.
15. Lloyd, *Martha Lloyd's Household Book*, pp. 33–4.
16. 1 October 1808, in *Letters*, p. 147.
17. Lloyd, *Martha Lloyd's Household Book*, p. 10.
18. 7 January 1807, in *Letters*, p. 119.
19. 27 December 1808, in *Letters*, pp. 166–7.
20. 6 June 1811, in *Letters*, p. 201.
21. *Northanger Abbey*, vol. 5 of *The Novels of Jane Austen*, p. 215.
22. Hannah Glasse, *The Art of Cookery Made Plain and Easy*, E. and J. Exshaw, Dublin, 1748, p. 19.
23. Lloyd, *Martha Lloyd's Household Book*, p. 17.
24. *Emma*, p. 172.
25. *c.* 2 March 1815, in *Letters*, p. 302.
26. 31 May 1811, in *Letters*, p. 200.
27. Ibid., p. 196.
28. 6 June 1811, in *Letters*, p. 202.
29. Lloyd, *Martha Lloyd's Household Book*, p. 97.
30. 31 May 1811, in *Letters*, p. 200.
31. 17 October 1815, in *Letters*, p. 303.
32. 23 September 1813, in *Letters*, p. 234.
33. 9 February 1813, in *Letters*, p. 215.
34. *Emma*, pp. 338–9.
35. 27 August 1805, in *Letters*, p. 114.
36. *Mansfield Park*, p. 387.
37. 16 September 1813, in *Letters*, p. 232.
38. Lloyd, *Martha Lloyd's Household Book*, p. [118].
39. 9 February 1813, in *Letters*, p. 214.
40. A long-term endocrine disorder in which the adrenal glands do not produce enough steroid hormones.
41. 24 January 1817, in *Letters*, p. 342.

Bibliography

PUBLISHED SOURCES

Austen, Caroline Mary Craven, *Reminiscences of Caroline Austen*, ed. Deirdre Le Faye, Jane Austen Society, Jane Austen's House, Chawton, Hampshire, 2004.

Austen, James Edward, *A Memoir of Jane Austen*, Richard Bentley & Son, London, 1871.

Austen, Jane, *The Novels of Jane Austen, 6 vols*, ed. R.W. Chapman, Oxford University Press, Oxford, 1988.

Austen, Jane, *Jane Austen: Collected Poems and Verse of the Austen Family*, ed. David Selwyn, Jane Austen Society and Fyfield Books, Manchester, 1996.

Austen, Jane, *Jane Austen's Later Manuscripts*, ed. Janet Todd and Linda Bree, Cambridge University Press, Cambridge, 2008.

Austen, Jane, *Jane Austen's Letters*, ed. Deirdre Le Faye, 4th edn, Oxford University Press, Oxford, 2011.

Austen-Leigh, Mary Augusta, *Personal Aspects of Jane Austen*, E.P. Dutton, New York, 1920.

Bell, John, *A New Catalogue of Bell's Circulating Library*, J. Bell, London, 1774.

Black, Maggie, and Deirdre Le Faye, *The Jane Austen Cookbook*, Chicago Review Press, Chicago, 1995.

Boosey, John, *A New Catalogue of the Circulating Library at No. 39, King Street, Cheapside*, J. Boosey, London, 1787.

Brears, Peter, *Report on Restoration of the Kitchen*, Jane Austen's House, Chawton, Hampshire, July 2004.

Campbell, Susan, *Walled Kitchen Gardens*, Shire Publications, Oxford, 2011.

Churchill, W.A., *Watermarks in Paper in Holland, England, France, etc., in the XVII and XVIII centuries and their interconnection*, Menno Hertzberger, Amsterdam, 1935.

Colquhoun, Kate, *Taste: The Story of Britain through Its Cooking*, Bloomsbury, London, 2007.

Dunning, Ronald, 'Jane Austen's Family', 2017, RootsWeb, wc.rootsweb.com/ trees/153642/I18/-/descendancy (accessed 27 August 2019).

Ellis, William, *The Country Housewife's Family Companion*, James Hodges, London, 1750.

Eveleigh, David J., *Old Cooking Utensils*, Shire Publications, Princes Risborough, 1997.

Fearn, Jacqueline, *Domestic Bygones*, Shire Publications, Oxford, 2010.

Gehrer, Julienne, *Dining with Jane Austen*, Ash Grove Press, Prairie Village KS, 2019.

Gisborne, Thomas, *An Enquiry into the Duties of the Female Sex*, T. Cadell & W. Davies, London, 1797.

Glasse, Hannah, *The Art of Cookery Made Plain and Easy*, E. & J. Exshaw, Dublin, 1748.

Glasse, Hannah, *The Complete Confectioner; or, Housekeeper's Guide*, West & Hughes, London, 1800.

Godmersham Park Guidebook, Godmersham Park Heritage Centre, Godmersham, 2003.

Herbst, Sharon Tyler and Ron, *The Cheese Lover's Companion*, HarperCollins, New York, 2007.

Hickman, Peggy, *A Jane Austen Household Book*, David & Charles, North Pomfret VT, 1977.

Hopkinson, David, 'The Later Life of Sir Francis Austen', *Collected Reports 1976–1985*, Jane Austen Society, Overton, 1989, pp. 253–9.

Lane, Maggie, *Jane Austen and Food*, Hambledon Press, London, 1995.

Le Faye, Deirdre, 'To dwell together in unity', *Collected Reports 1986–1995*, Jane Austen Society, Alton, 1997, pp. 151–63.

Le Faye, Deirdre, 'Anna Lefroy and Her Austen Family Letters,' *Princeton University Library Chronicle*, vol. 62, no. 3, Spring 2001, pp. 519–62.

Le Faye, Deirdre, *Jane Austen: A Family Record*, Cambridge University Press, Cambridge, 2004.

Le Faye, Deirdre, *A Chronology of Jane Austen and Her Family: 1600–2000*, Cambridge University Press, Cambridge, 2006.

Le Faye, Deirdre, *Jane Austen's Steventon*, Jane Austen Society, Jane Austen's House, Chawton, Hampshire, 2007.

Le Faye, Deirdre, *Jane Austen's Country Life*, Frances Lincoln, London, 2014.

Lillie, Nicola and Marilyn Yurdan, *Lavender Water & Snail Syrup: Miss Ambler's Household Book of Georgian Cures and Remedies*, History Press, Stroud, 2013.

Markham, Gervase, *The English Huswife*, Roger Jackson, London, 1615.

Mason, Charlotte, *The Lady's Assistant for Regulating and Supplying the Table*, J. Walter, London, 1787.

Mescher, Virginia, 2005, '"How Sweet It Is!" A History of Sugar and Sugar Refining in the United States', Ragged Soldier, raggedsoldier.com/sugar_history.pdf (accessed 11 May 2019).

Montagu, Belinda, *To the Manor Born: Lady Montagu of Beaulieu*, Gentry Books, London, 1971.

Raffald, Elizabeth, *The Experienced English Housekeeper*, R. Baldwin, London, 1769.

Shaw, Carolyn, *Cooks and Quakers: 200 Years of a Family's Recipe Books*, Quacks Books, York, 2016.

Smith, Ben, *Jane Austen's Homecoming: Chawton 1809*, Trail Publishing, Newcastle upon Tyne, n.d.

Smith, Eliza, *The Compleat Housewife*, J. Pemberton, London, 1727.

The Whole Duty of a Woman, *c.* 1700, British Library Digital Store 14477.a.38.

Tucker, George Holbert, 'Jane Austen's Topaz Cross', *Collected Reports 1976–1985*, Jane Austen Society, Overton, 1989, pp. 76–7.

Vick, Robin, 'A Tourist's View of Southampton and Portsmouth in 1811', *Collected Reports 1996–2000*, Jane Austen Society, Bristol, 2005, pp, 38–40.

Whatman, Susanna, *The Housekeeping Book of Susanna Whatman 1776–1800*, Random Century and National Trust, London, 1987.

Woodforde, James, *A Country Parson: James Woodforde's Diary 1759–1802*, Tiger Books, London, 1991.

UNPUBLISHED SOURCES

Austen, Edward, *Stewardship accounts for the estate of Edward Austen, later Edward Knight esquire, 1809-1819, Bradley Trimmer of Alton, solicitors*, Hampshire Record Office, Winchester.

Austen-Leigh Family Archive, Hampshire Record Office, Winchester.

Austen, Martha, Letter from Gosport to Revd J.E. Austen, Tring Park, Hertfordshire, 30 September 1828, Collection of Freydis Welland, Vancouver BC.

Austen, Mary, *Diary Kept by Mary Austen, 1836*, Austen-Leigh Family Archive, Hampshire Record Office, Winchester.

Jane Austen's House Museum Archive, Hampshire Record Office, Winchester.

Jervoise Family of Herriard estate and personal accounts, *c.* 1660s–1720s, Hampshire Record Office, Winchester.

Knight Family, *The Knight Family Cookbook*, *c.* 1793 Chawton House Library, Chawton, Hampshire.

Le Faye, Deirdre, 'Martha Lloyd Recipe Book: Notes on Watermark', Chawton House Library, Chawton, Hampshire, *c.* 1990.

Lloyd, Martha, *Martha Lloyd's Household Book*, *c.* 1796, Jane Austen's House, Chawton, Hampshire.

T.E. Carpenter Letters Archive, Jane Austen's House, Chawton, Hampshire, 1953–1956.

Picture credits

Index

Page numbers in *italics* indicate facsimile images